Ordinary Women
Extraordinary

PRACTICAL INSIGHTS
from WOMEN OF
THE BIBLE

God

Dedication

———◦◦◦◦———

*T*his book is lovingly dedicated to Kay Smith: our sister, our friend, our mentor, our co-laborer, and our pastor's wife. We have learned so much from this extraordinary woman and we are eternally grateful.

—June Hesterly and Sandy MacIntosh

Acknowledgments

We would like to, first of all, thank each of the women who have contributed a message to this volume, and it is our prayer that the Lord will abundantly bless them for sharing their ministry with us.

Thank you to Christine Scheller who worked tirelessly to help transform these wonderful spoken messages into written form. Without all your work this book would not have been possible.

To Romy Godding, Cristin Novak, Anna Hamp, Sarah Yardley, and Nawal Zabaneh—thank you for your proofreading and editing assistance; and, to Carol Gill for your help with transcription.

To Aric Everson, thank you for creating an incredible cover; and to Bob Bubnis for your quick, but patient work on the layout.

And finally to June Hesterly and Sandy MacIntosh, thank you for allowing us to work alongside you in bringing to fruition the vision and burden the Lord placed upon your hearts for this book.

As you read these messages, it is our desire that you would see more clearly just how extraordinary our God is!

—Calvary Chapel Publishing

Contents

Introduction

*D*o you ever feel ordinary? The Bible is filled with wonderful and fascinating stories of ordinary women like you and me who became extraordinary in the hands of God. Not all of the women in these stories are perfect or successful. In fact some are flawed and full of mistakes to avoid—like Job's wife, whose words multiplied her husband's suffering; and, Euodia and Syntyche, whose inability to get along is recorded for all time. But many give us examples worthy to follow—like Mary of Bethany, whose lifestyle of worship is an inspiration; and, Rahab, whose simple faith led to the salvation of her entire family, and to her placement in the lineage of Jesus Christ.

It is our hope and prayer that this book will be used to remind you of the love, patience, and power of our extraordinary God. It is Him that we want you to see. It is Him that we wish to portray and glorify. It is Him that we need. All of us long to live effective lives. Because we love and serve such an extraordinary God, He is ready to meet us and transform us into extraordinary women to be used by Him.

His hands await us.

—Sandy MacIntosh and June Hesterly

—⚬⚬⚬—

Growing in the knowledge of God is the most important pursuit you can undertake in your life. It should be your life's goal.

—Sandy MacIntosh

—⚬⚬⚬—

A Woman of the Word or a Woman of the World?

by Sandy MacIntosh

Of every tree of the garden you may freely eat; but of the tree of the knowledge of good and evil you shall not eat, for in the day that you eat of it you shall surely die.
—Genesis 2:16–17

Genesis chapter 3 may be the most pivotal chapter in the entire Bible. Nothing is ever the same after the events recorded in its twenty-four verses, and yet, it is in this chapter that God begins to put His incredible, marvelous, self-sacrificing plan for the redemption of creation into action. One commentator said that the events that take place in chapter 3 are the most far-reaching events in the history of the world and certainly in the history of the church.

I hope when you read this chapter you don't think, *Eve was so stupid; I'd never do anything like that,* because her story is about you and me as much as it is about Eve. We possess the same character, the same nature, and the same weaknesses that she had. Genesis chapter 3 is full of spiritual truth and great realities of the Christian life. It teaches us about temptation, sin, punishment, and redemption. To understand it is to better understand ourselves, our Enemy, and our need for a Savior.

Years ago we studied the heroes and well-known people of the book of Genesis in our women's Bible study at Horizon

Christian Fellowship. We called the study *Ordinary People, Extraordinary God* because we studied ordinary men and women like Abraham and Sarah that God, through His power, transformed into extraordinary men and women. This is a story about an extraordinary woman who, because of her own stupidity, became very ordinary.

First of all, Eve was absolutely extraordinary physically. She was not born, but was created by God's own hands. Therefore, she was perfect—the fulfillment of every woman's dream of what she would like to see in the mirror. In the garden of Eden, there was no death and no aging process, and there were no environmental hazards or fattening foods. Eve never had any reason to frown with frustration or develop a poor self-image. She faced no competition. Physically, she was unlike any other woman who has ever lived.

Second, Eve lived in the most extraordinary place, a garden that God had planted with His own hands. God did not speak the garden into existence; He planted it. It was beautiful and weed free. It provided a satisfying variety of foods. There was no rain or bad weather in Eve's environment, just a soft mist that watered the garden every night, keeping everything moist and lush. Her natural surroundings were perfect.

Third, Eve was personally extraordinary. It was impossible for her to make a mistake about whom to marry. Adam was the right man because he was the only man. Wouldn't that have simplified things incredibly? She had no past. She had made no bad choices. She had no parents, no in-laws, no siblings, and no old boyfriends to raise their hands and accuse her of anything. She had no life experiences. She didn't have a difficult childhood. She didn't go through puberty. She was created by God's hands as a perfect woman.

Fourth, she was extraordinary spiritually—she had a perfect relationship with God. There is an ancient saying, *The best fertilizer a garden can have is the footprint of the gardener.* And in this garden, the Chief Gardener walked and talked with her every afternoon.

In summary, Eve was an extraordinary woman: she had it all physically; she had it all naturally; she had it all personally; and she had it all spiritually. Amazingly, "having it all" was not enough for her. The reason it wasn't enough is because she was like you and me, and we are like her. Kay Smith refers to her mindset as the *Eve Mentality.* It comes from discontent and from asking "Why?" all the time. It comes from deciding to listen to that voice inside your head that says, *I know what's right and best for me,* or that louder voice that says, *You're not the boss of me!* or that little voice that says, *You don't understand me,* or the one that whispers, *Just this much, just this once, just one little bite.* It is that voice of dissatisfaction that speaks loudly and often interrupts the beauty and simplicity of God's Word in our lives. The *Eve Mentality* caused her to go from extraordinary to ordinary.

Consider the scene in which this story is played out. Scripture says the tree was in the center of the garden. Sin is always available right in the middle of our lives. Eve could look at the tree. She could walk by it. She could smell it. She could talk about it. She could think about it. It was right in the center of the garden, and the opportunity to sin was always readily available.

Although Eve had all that she needed, she was discontented, and began to do the one thing that you and I should never do— she began to converse with the Enemy, who appeared to her as a beautiful serpent. I don't think Eve planned to seek him out. Her downfall began innocently with a conversation. How often in my life failure starts with my mouth—with a conversation I shouldn't have had or words I shouldn't have spoken.

The Serpent must have looked different from all the other animals in the entire kingdom that God had shown to Adam. When Eve first saw him, rather than doing what Scripture tells us to do and fleeing from the Enemy, she yielded to him and lost everything. Someone has rightly said, *Nothing is more remarkable than Satan's powerlessness to overcome you apart from your own consent.*

God's instructions were simple: *Of every tree of the garden you may freely eat; but of the tree of the knowledge of good and evil you shall not eat, for in the day that you eat of it you shall surely die* (verses 16–17). He spoke only a few words, but they were very clear. Because this instruction was given to Adam, it is tempting to think that he never passed the information on to Eve. In my household, I am the last to know anything. I sometimes have to go to church on Sunday morning to find out where Mike is going or hear about where he has been. I know what it is like to live in a relationship where information is not free flowing. I don't think that was the case with Eve, and we can't blame Adam for not telling her what God had said.

In chapter 3, verse 1, the Serpent said the same three words to Eve that he said to Jesus when he tempted Him in the wilderness: *Has God said?* Have you ever gotten into the middle of a situation and thought, *I wonder if God really said that? I wonder if God really meant that? Certainly, He is not that strict or overbearing. He didn't really say that.* That is always how temptation begins. Notice that the Serpent didn't come to her and say, *Eve, why don't you bow down to me? I would be a better god than the One who walks in the garden with you.* He didn't say, *God's a liar. Don't trust anything He says.* He probably spoke to her in a sweet, syrupy voice: *Let's have a reasonable conversation here. Has God indeed said, "You shall not eat of every tree of the garden"?* (see 3:1)

This isn't what God had said, or even close to what God had said. His proclamation was, *Of every tree of the garden you may freely eat*

(2:16). Right from the beginning, Satan seduced Eve into doubting God's love for her. She made a huge mistake in listening to him because he was very cunning in his approach. In verse 2, Eve repeated back to him what she thought God had said: *We may eat the fruit of the trees of the garden.* But what did she leave out? The word *freely!* She understated God's generous provision, and the privilege that was available to her in the garden.

In verse 3, she misquoted God again by saying that the tree was in the midst of the garden. Had God said, *In the midst of the garden?* No! That is not what He had said at all. Satan's strategy was to cast doubt on God's Word and plant in her uncertainty about His goodness: *Are you restricted from eating from every tree in this delightful place? You poor darling; you must be so hungry. All this fruit just hanging there and God won't let you have any of it?* The truth of the matter is that God gave liberally of every tree in the garden—every tree but one. Rather than talking about the abundance of God's provision, Satan harped on this one restriction. He does that to us because he doesn't want us to think for a minute about how lavishly God has blessed us. He wants to make us worry about one little restriction that rubs us the wrong way.

Before Satan came along, the Tree of the Knowledge of Good and Evil was probably just an ordinary tree to Eve, but he aroused her curiosity. Her first mistake was entering into a conversation with the Serpent. Her second mistake was entertaining curiosity about God's restriction. Eve began to see this tree as Satan wanted her to see it. Right then, she should have done what James 4:7 says: *Resist the devil and he will flee from you.* Because she submitted to him, he came with more and more temptation, which he does in our lives as well.

Eve's description of the tree was not the same as God's. She failed to identify the tree for what it was. She didn't talk about its substance, but only talked about its location. God had clearly stated that it was the Tree of the Knowledge of Good and Evil. It had the ability to make her wise about things she didn't need to be wise about. Up to that point, even though Eve had the propensity to sin within her character, she had no knowledge of evil.

I always wanted to see the movie, *Schindler's List*, because the Holocaust has always fascinated me. But my husband and I don't go to R-rated movies so I waited to see it until the edited version appeared on television. It is an awesome story, but one full of evil deeds. Watching it was sort of like feasting on the Tree of the Knowledge of Good and Evil for me. I don't think I got a full night's sleep for six weeks afterwards because all the atrocities committed against the Jews played over and over again in my mind as I lay in bed at night. Even though it communicated a strong moral lesson about how the forces of good can overcome evil, my thoughts were consumed with the horror of it all. This tree imparted that kind of knowledge of good and evil to Eve. God's warning was meant to protect her; it had purpose in her life.

Next, she said, *God has said, "You shall not eat it, nor shall you touch it"* (verse 3). That isn't what God had said. She added the word *touch* to God's instructions. Now we can see her mind working: *I can't have the fruit on this tree, I can't even touch it.* She was overcome by self-pity. Do you ever think like that—*God is so unfair?*

The last words that Eve said were *lest you die* (verse 3). *Lest* is a word that means "it might happen." For example, someone might say, *Hurry up, lest we be late.* God had declared, *You shall surely die* (Genesis 2:17). Judgment was definite according to God. He had told them that it would happen *in that day* (see verse 17). Spiritual mortality set in the very moment she took and ate of the tree. Satan knew what would happen to Eve, and he wanted her to succumb and lose the immortality she possessed in the garden. Do you realize that if Adam and Eve had not been disobedient, they would have lived forever? Mortality is a result of their sin.

Notice that when the Serpent responded to Eve in verse 4, he said, *You will not surely die.* Even the Serpent knew that the word was *surely*, not *lest*. Satan knows God's Word and trembles at it. If you think he is ignorant about Scripture, you are mistaken because he's got it down! He inserted one simple word, the woman believed it, and the world was changed and lost until Jesus came. Satan then said, *God knows that in the day you eat of it your eyes will be opened, and you will be like God, knowing good and evil.* This was his sinful rebellion from the very beginning. He wanted to be like God. In fact, he wanted to be lifted up higher than God.

The commandment was clear and concise. Because Satan caused Eve to doubt God's Word, she got with his program. First, she understated God's provision. She left out the word *freely* when describing what she was permitted to eat. Second, she overstated God's prohibition. He hadn't said that she could not *touch* the tree. Third, she understated His judgment. God had said she would *surely* die if she ate of the fruit. The handling of God's Word is so important. God's Word tells us to take nothing from it, to add nothing to it, and to change nothing in it (Revelation 22:18). She failed in all three directives. We can be absolutely certain that mishandling the Word of God leads to trouble.

Eve then made another mistake. She should have run to ask Adam exactly what God had said, or gone to the place where God had met her in the garden and asked Him to clarify His instructions. She didn't do either of those things. There was no hesitation as the Serpent enticed her to take the fruit. She looked at it, liked it, and ate it. The tempted became the tempter when she then took the fruit to her husband. Don't ever think that you sin alone, or that it only affects you, or that you can keep it a secret and nobody will find out. Eventually sin begins to affect everyone, and the consequences are like the ripples from a stone thrown into a pond—they go on and on.

Sin is simply reclaiming my right to myself from God. Hosea 10:13 says, *You have eaten the fruit of lies, because you trusted in your own way.* That's what Eve did. She chose her own way. We never sin *in spite* of ourselves. We sin *because* of ourselves and that forbidden fruit. I don't know what the forbidden fruit is in your life. Perhaps it's TV, movies, magazines, or soap operas. God's restrictions for Adam and Eve were meant for their protection. The same is true for us.

Don't get into an argument with Satan. He is subtle and clever. Do what the New Testament says: resist him and flee (James 4:7). Don't be afraid to simply turn your back and run from temptation. I'm not the strongest person in the world. I cannot stand there and figure the whole thing out. I need to turn around and get out of a tempting situation, and that is what you need to do too. We also need to practice saying the word *no.* Spend some time in the next week standing in front of the mirror saying no to yourself, then turn around, leave, and come back to the mirror and do it again. We don't have enough practice denying ourselves. We don't resist temptation. We don't run from sin. We don't say no to the simple things in our lives that take us away from God. If, at the very beginning, Eve had looked the Serpent in the face, said no, and gotten out of there, we would not have the problems that we do today.

Verses 6–7 describe the pivotal moment in human history when everything was forever changed: *So when the woman saw that the tree was good for food, that it was pleasant to the eyes, and a tree desirable to*

*make one wise, she took of its fruit and ate. She also gave to her husband with her,
and he ate. Then the eyes of both of them were opened, and they knew that they
were naked, and they sewed fig leaves together and made themselves coverings.*

This was not the first time Eve had looked at the tree. It was
in the garden every day. She looked at it again and saw that physically it was good for food; aesthetically, it was pleasant to look
at; and intellectually, it would make her wise. Her flesh lusted
after it, her eyes longed for it, and her pride coveted it. Then she
took of it. First John 2:16 says that the lust of the eyes, the lust
of the flesh, and the pride of life are the three things that trip us
up and cause us to sin. It is always the same. Satan has no new
tricks. He comes to you and me in the same way. Sin never
appeals to the spirit, but always to the flesh.

Next came division between Eve and her husband, discord
between God and man, and defeat for humanity. But victory came
for Satan. The repercussions are evident all the way through the
Bible. The consequences were many and terrible. The first was guilt
as they experienced shame for the first time. Because of that shame,
they covered themselves. They not only saw themselves naked, but
their mortality was also exposed. Their physical bodies were no
longer eternal. I think the minute they ate of the fruit, the beauty
they had known was replaced by decay. Perhaps wrinkles and sag-
ging appeared immediately.

The second consequence was fear. They hid from God and
from each other. The old days of innocence, fellowship, and walking and talking in the garden face-to-face with God were gone.
They were afraid to see Him. The third consequence was judgment. It is so amazing that even though they were hiding from
God, even though they saw their sin and mortality, and the decay
that had begun to set in, God did not hide from them. He looked
for them, called out to them, and provided for them. But when

He found them, He also had to judge them because He is a God of justice, and He had sufficiently warned them. He was bound to His Word.

So guilt came, fear came, and judgment came—but the worst consequence of their sin must have been the separation they experienced from God because it was now impossible for Adam and Eve to remain in the garden. Sin and paradise are not compatible. Isaiah wrote, *Your iniquities have separated you from your God* (59:2). They were driven out and a guard was placed at the door. One commentator said that if they had eaten from the Tree of Life once they were mortal, they would have lived in their sin forever. In order to keep them from the Tree of Life, God sent them outside of the garden, and death became their only hope.

These horrible, horrible consequences have spanned from that day until now. However, consistent with God's character, judgment always comes with a promise. In the wake of their sin, God made the first of His covenants with them. He told Eve that her Seed would bruise the head of the Serpent, and that someday a Savior would come. Even though Genesis is about the beginning of creation, it is also about the beginning of sorrow. It is about the burdensome curse of going from life to death. If you can't wait for the happy ending to this story, go straight to the book of Revelation, which promises us that there is a place where there will be no more sorrow, no more curse, no more death, and no more separation from God. The plan that God put into action immediately after the fall provided a Savior for Eve and Adam, and for you and me as well. Now aren't those the things you want to know about? I want to know about those things.

I absolutely love the Olympics. I watched them as a child and I am still fascinated by the quest of the athletes—by their dedication, discipline, and determination. They put everything else on hold for years in order to excel at their sport. While the competition might take a minute or two, it takes four, eight, and sometimes many more years to prepare for those brief minutes. I want that kind of devotion in my spiritual life.

I'm so un-athletic, but I would have loved to have been an Olympic athlete and known that kind of discipline. I discovered my sport watching the Winter Olympics in 2002. I think I could have competed in the luge race! You just get on and you don't even have to pay attention to where you're going. There was a competitor close to my age from Japan called Grandma Luge. I told my daughter I thought I could pursue this sport and she said, *You know, Mom, I think I've almost outgrown the feeling that I could be embarrassed by my parents.* She might be challenged in this if I were to become the next Grandma Luge!

Seriously though, all the time, agony, and pain that athletes expend as they pursue their goals can come to nothing in a millisecond if they lose. How much time do you spend knowing the One you will spend eternity with? How dedicated are you? How disciplined are you? Do you have the *Eve Mentality?* It is so contrary to the gospel. It is the mindset that says, *Me first—I know what is right for me; I know what fulfills me; I want to express myself and assert myself; I want everyone to know who I am; I want to defend myself; I want to be free from any restrictions in my life.* Jesus asks us to die to ourselves and live for Him. R. A. Torrey said, *He waits to be wanted.*[1]

I hope you are aware that Satan is the same today as he was in the beginning. He is right here like a ferocious lion seeking ways to devour you. He would love to take your Christian witness, your Christian family, your love of the Word, your love of

---

[1] Torrey, R. A. "WatchCry Quotes." Posted February 9, 2003. *Revival Resource Center.* www.watchword.org. (Accessed August 9, 2004.)

Christian fellowship, even your love of God Himself, and dilute it and deceive you in order to defeat you. Remember, Satan didn't tell Eve she would no longer have a relationship with God. He would love for you to remain a Christian, and go to church and Bible study, but live a life of sin. He would love it because the most powerful thing he can do is to have you call yourself a Christian but not live like one—to have you talk to Christians like you were a Christian, but talk differently in the workplace. That is his goal and plan for you. God has provided everything that you need in His Word and in the fellowship that you have with Him, yet Satan is still after you.

Eve had absolutely everything that she needed in order to win this battle. She had God's Word, but she disregarded it. She had fellowship with God, but she neglected it. She had fellowship with her husband, but obviously, she rejected it. She had someone to turn to for counsel and help. She lived in the beautiful, incredible, glorious garden with wonderful food and a wonderful man that God had provided, and still she was seduced into believing it wasn't enough.

You and I live in a fallen world. We are much more susceptible to the wiles of the Enemy than Eve was. Cynthia Heald said, *There is a restlessness deep within each of us that compels us to search for the person, the place, the job, the "god" that will fill the void and give us peace. This restlessness drives us to find someone who will love us for who we are, understand our fears and anxieties, affirm our worth, and call our lives into account. To admit our need and dependence upon God requires humility and vulnerability which paves the way for knowing God and also for being intimate with Him.*[2]

When Pablo Casals reached the age of ninety-five, a young reporter threw him a question: *Mr. Casals, you are ninety-five and the greatest cellist who ever lived. Why do you still practice six hours a day?* Pablo

---

[2] Heald, Cynthia. *Intimacy with God.* Colorado Springs: Navpress, 2000.

Casals answered, *Because I think I'm making progress!* [3] I don't how spiritually mature you are, but you should be working just as hard to know the Lord today as you did when you first found Him. Growing in the knowledge of God is the most important pursuit you can undertake in your life. It should be your life's goal.

The Psalmist cried out, *That I might know You,* and, *When He said "Seek my face," I sought His face* (see Psalm 27:8). God is saying to you right now, *Seek My face.* Respond by declaring, *Your face I will seek. I want to know You. I want to give You all my time and all my interests and pursuits that I might know You.* Paul said, *I also count all things loss for the excellence of the knowledge of Christ Jesus my Lord* (Philippians 3:8).

My prayer is that you will now feel quickened in your spirit with a need to know God more than you have ever known Him before. This desire should be followed by a decision to simplify your life, to clean out those things that distract you or displease God, and your decision must be followed by determination. Every power in the universe that is opposed to God will come against you and your desire to know Him. Everything on TV will be better than it ever was before. Every phone conversation will be a temptation. Obstacles and distractions are going to come at you and confuse you unless you are determined to order your life. Psalm 46:10 says, *Be still, and know that I am God.* Quiet the unnecessary busyness in your life. Find a place and time to have intimate fellowship with God. Listen to Him, learn from Him, and lean on Him. Love on Him and be loved by Him. Become a student of His Word. Be devoted to it. Finally, there is one thing I know: Once I was blind but now I see. A life of devotion begins as simply as that.

---

[3] "Pablo Casals." Posted July 16, 1999. *The Sermon Illustrator. www.sermonillustrator.org.* (Accessed August 15, 2004.)

Reflections

1. Reflect for a moment on the impact Eve's life made upon all of mankind.
2. How was this extraordinary woman transformed into an ordinary one?
3. Why is it vitally important to guard yourself from having an *Eve Mentality*?
4. Describe the mistakes Eve made concerning the Serpent and the Word of God?
5. What practical steps can you take to arm yourself with a sure and working knowledge of God's Word in order to avoid her path?
6. The consequences of Eve's sin brought death not only to herself and Adam, but to the entire human race. However, God has made provision for salvation through His Son, Jesus Christ. If you already know Him, take a moment to offer praise and thanksgiving for the wonderful gift of salvation. If you have not yet received Him, take this time to surrender your life and receive salvation from your sin and new life in Him.

About the Author

Sandy MacIntosh is the wife of Mike MacIntosh, a pastor and evangelist with a vision to win people to Jesus Christ, disciple them in Christ, and send them out for Christ. Sandy surrendered her heart and life to Jesus Christ over thirty years ago in Corona del Mar, California.

Sandy's husband, Mike, is the pastor of Horizon Christian Fellowship in San Diego, California. Over one hundred churches and para-church organizations worldwide have grown out of this congregation. Sandy has spoken evangelistically and as an encouragement to pastors' wives and women across the United States and the world. She currently teaches two weekly women's Bible studies at Horizon. Sandy attended Stephen's College and Long Beach State University.

Sandy and Mike live in San Diego and have five children and fourteen grandchildren.

If you forget everything else,
please let this be carved upon
your mind and heart:
God is available to help you. In fact,
He is your only real source of help.

—Kay Smith

Hannah

A Woman of Prayer

by Kay Smith

And she was in bitterness of soul, and prayed unto the LORD,
and wept sore.
—I Samuel 1:10, KJV

Have you ever been in the midst of a painful trial and someone delighted to rub salt in that wound? Hannah was an Old Testament saint who struggled in one of the most heartbreaking situations a woman can encounter: she was unable to bear children. Not only was she infertile, but her husband's second wife delighted to irritate that deep, deep hurt. Hannah triumphed over her adversary because she knew what to do and where to go with her sorrow.

Hannah's story begins in I Samuel 1:1–7: *Now there was a certain man of Ramathaim-zophim, of mount Ephraim [near Bethlehem], and his name was Elkanah, the son of Jeroham, the son of Elihu, the son of Tohu, the son of Zuph, an Ephrathite: And he had two wives; the name of the one was Hannah, and the name of the other Peninnah: and Peninnah had children, but Hannah had no children. And this man went up out of his city yearly to worship and to sacrifice unto the LORD of hosts in Shiloh. And the two sons of Eli, Hophni and Phinehas, the priests of the LORD, were there. And when the time was that Elkanah offered, he gave to Peninnah his wife, and to all her sons and her daughters, portions: But unto Hannah he gave a worthy portion; for he loved Hannah: but the LORD had shut up her womb. And her adversary also provoked her sore, for to make her fret, because the LORD had shut up her womb. And as he did so year by year, when she went up to the house of the LORD, so she provoked her; therefore she wept, and did not eat* (KJV).

We see in this passage that Hannah was continually provoked by her adversary. *Provoke* means "to incite to anger." Have you ever been provoked by an adversary? Verse 6 says that the adversary provoked her *sore, for to make her fret,* and in my marginal reference it says, *The adversary angered her.* According to the *New International Version,* her adversary *kept provoking her in order to irritate her,* and the *Amplified Bible* explains that *her rival provoked her greatly to vex her.* Peninnah did it maliciously to make Hannah angry and upset.

Hannah's adversary provoked her as she went to the house of the Lord. Isn't it strange that our adversary will often seek to provoke us as we go to the house of the Lord? Have you ever had that happen? You've started out for church with your mouth filled with laughter and your heart with joy, and then, all of a sudden, everything comes in on you. The adversary loves to provoke us as we are on our way to the house of the Lord.

Hannah's heart was so grieved that her husband began to notice that she was weeping and not eating. When we cannot eat because of the adversary's vexing, it is usually because we are hurting very deeply.

Verses 8–10 describe her state of mind: *Then said Elkanah her husband to her, Hannah, why weepest thou? and why eatest thou not? and why is thy heart grieved? am not I better to thee than ten sons? So Hannah rose up after they had eaten in Shiloh, and after they had drunk. Now Eli the priest sat upon a seat by a post of the temple of the LORD. And she was in bitterness of soul, and prayed unto the LORD, and wept sore* (KJV).

Elkanah was concerned about his wife, but he was unable to alleviate her suffering. In verse 11 she asks the Lord to look on her affliction. One translation calls it her *sorrow,* and another calls it her *misery.* Doesn't that paint a black picture? In verse 15, we learn that she called herself a *woman of sorrowful spirit*. The *New International Version* says, *I am a woman who is deeply troubled*. Have you ever felt that way? Have you ever been a woman of sorrowful spirit?

Hannah's barrenness was a great burden, but she was made miserable by Penninah's taunting. We can bear a lot of things if we're not provoked by an adversary. But when that provocation comes in to make us fret and to make us irritable and angry, our situation can seem unbearable. Have you ever been very patient in a trial until the adversary started putting thoughts into your mind, and suddenly all patience was gone, and you felt as though you couldn't bear it one more minute?

In verse 16, Hannah said that she was speaking out of the abundance of her complaint and grief. She was not just experiencing a little grief, but great grief. The *Amplified Bible* says, *Out of my great complaint and bitter provocation I have been speaking*. Bitter provocation, anguish, misery, a sorrowful spirit, affliction, grief—truly Hannah was a woman who was suffering. A variety of things can happen to us when we are in a state of such sorrow and anguish. The very deep hurt affected her mentally, emotionally, and physically.

I want us to see ourselves in Hannah, a handmaiden of the Lord, and a woman whose name means "gracious." Hannah handled her trials with tremendous grace, but she was weighted down by anguish of spirit. Sometimes when we're weighted down by sorrow, and our adversary starts to provoke us, we think, *God doesn't love me*, or, *I'm not His handmaiden anymore. He really doesn't care. I've done something terrible and He has turned His back on me and forgotten me*. But that's not true. Even His most precious handmaidens go through deep anguish of heart.

Any situation or circumstance that brings us to the place of distress and bitterness of soul is ultimately because of the provocation of the adversary, Satan. When we end up irritated, angry, upset, and mentally distressed, Satan is in it as an adversary trying to cause us to fall. He wants us to become so discouraged that we give up. As we understand how we are provoked and the result of that provocation, we will discover why it is so important that we learn from Hannah's example.

What do you do when you are vexed by the adversary? Hannah truly was gracious in her response to Peninnah. She didn't turn around and shout, *Oh, be quiet, Peninnah!* Some people respond in anger, but our answer should be gracious. Other people pull back into a sullen silence. Have you ever been with that kind of person? They won't talk, and they are usually a little bit self-righteous and smug. There are times when people are so wounded that they can't talk, but a healthy person deals with problems. The unhealthy person bottles up his or her anger. This is a defense mechanism that really doesn't work well because anger is eventually going to be expressed someplace. If it isn't expressed with a husband, it will erupt with the children, the dog, or the next-door neighbor. Some people take counsel from the ungodly. Psalm 1:1 says, *Blessed is the man that walketh not in the counsel of the ungodly* (KJV). Don't go to that unsaved friend or even to the immature Christian for advice. When you are provoked by your adversary, don't get ungodly counsel. Others turn back to the path they walked before they knew Jesus and thus alienate themselves from the only real source of help.

Let's look at what Hannah did, and in seeing what Hannah did, we'll gain insight into what we should do. First Samuel 1:11 says that she *vowed a vow, and said, O LORD of hosts, if thou wilt indeed look on the affliction of thine handmaid, and remember me, and not forget thine handmaid, but wilt give unto thine handmaid a man child, then I will give him unto the LORD all the days of his life, and there shall no razor come upon his head* (KJV).

First, Hannah went to the only real source of help—our God. Isn't that precious? She left Elkanah at the table, probably with Peninnah and all their little kids, and headed for the tabernacle. Hannah poured out her sorrows before the Lord instead of reacting in anger towards those around her. Scripture doesn't record her throwing plates and food at her rival, and it doesn't record Hannah complaining to Elkanah, *Hey, tell her to be quiet. She's driving me crazy. It's unfair.* She didn't cry and carry on, *I can't bear this any longer.* Instead, she went to the place of help. She went to the tabernacle.

Let the tabernacle in the story of Hannah represent your place of prayer. When you're provoked by the adversary, head for the place of prayer. Therein is your help. Fortunately we can pray anytime and anywhere. I like to have a place of prayer in my home that's all my own. It's that secret place where I kneel before God and cry out to Him, telling Him everything that's on my heart. I can confess how rotten I've been, and He understands and still loves me. We all need a place where we can absolutely unload everything.

To have bitterness of soul or spirit is not a good thing. Hannah was able to go before the Lord and say, *Lord, I can't stand this woman. She's driving me crazy with her constant provocations!* Do you know you can do that? You can go before the Lord and say, *Lord, I can't handle it. I don't have the strength to handle it. Please, work out a solution to this!*

Why does God want you to go to Him? Because in His Word He promises to help you, no matter what circumstance you are in or what pathway you are walking down. If you forget everything else, please let this be carved upon your mind and heart: God is available to help you. In fact, He is your only real source of help. First Peter 5:7 tells us to cast, not just a part of our care, but *all* of our care upon Him because He cares for us. Have you ever stopped in the middle of a horrible problem and realized, *God cares for me?* That blesses me so much because one of the things Satan constantly tries to tell me is: *God doesn't even see you. He doesn't even care. He's not interested.*

In her prayer, Hannah said, *Remember me* (1 Samuel 1:11). At that moment she may not have been entirely conscious of the fact that God cared for her. Even David said, *Hear me, LORD. Awaken to my cause. Arouse Yourself to deliver me.* It's as though he thought God had forgotten him. Some of the other prophets—Jeremiah, for example—asked, *Lord, have You forgotten me?*

Psalm 55:22 says, *Cast thy burden upon the LORD, and he shall sustain thee* (KJV). Cast your burden on the Lord, and He will care for you and sustain you. What does *sustain* mean? It means to "hold you steady in the problem." He'll hold you steady in your situation. In *The Living Bible*, 1 Peter 5:1 says to let Him have our worries and cares because He is always thinking about us and watching everything that concerns us. Isn't that precious? Remember the old chorus, *Take your burden to the Lord and leave it there?* Don't take it back on your shoulders, but leave it there!

Psalm 37:5 has sustained me through many, many trials. It's a Scripture that I fall back on continually. It says that we are to commit our way unto Him. That doesn't just mean our problems. It means we are to commit our entire lives and all our circumstances to Him, and He will bring everything to the conclusion that will bring glory to His name. He'll take complete charge of the situation. We simply need to move out of the way and let Him work.

I was amused one day listening to a preacher on the radio as I curled my hair. He was talking about marriage and he said submission for the wife is simply ducking out of the way so God can hit her husband. I think submission is much gentler than that, but he was giving us a mental picture to help us. Committing our way unto the Lord involves the same principle. We are moving out of the way, saying, *God, You take control,* so that He can work in our life.

James 5:13 instructs those who are suffering to pray. Are you being ill-treated? Are you suffering evil today? You should pray. Are you afflicted today? Pray. That's what God wanted Hannah to do, and that's what He wants you to do. God promises in 1 Peter 3:12, *The eyes of the Lord are over the righteous, and his ears are open unto their prayers* (KJV). Remember that—God's eyes are open to the righteous. The word *righteous* isn't referring to the person that is sinless, but to the one who is in right standing with God through the blood of Jesus Christ. If you're in right standing with God through Jesus' blood, His eyes are upon you and His ears are open to your prayers.

Hannah told Eli she had poured out her soul before the Lord. Have you ever poured out your soul before the Lord? In Psalm 62:7–8, David says, *God is my salvation and my glory: the rock of my strength, and my refuge.* And then he says, *Trust in him at all times* (KJV). Why? Because God was his salvation, his rock of strength, and his refuge.

The adversary can provoke us through people or circumstances, but we have a refuge in God if we will run and hide ourselves in Him. He wants to protect us; He wants to overshadow us; He wants to take control of the situation; and, He wants to deliver us from that which is destroying us. He will do all these things if we let Him because He is faithful.

Psalm 46:1 says, *God is our refuge and strength, a very present help in trouble* (KJV). Was He just a present help for Hannah? No. He's a help for us, too. I wonder if God goes around the earth saying, *Who will turn to Me that I can show Myself strong on her behalf today? Who will turn her life over completely so I can move on her behalf and receive glory for the miracles I'm going to perform in these situations?*

Vain is the help of man, Psalm 108:12 tells us. God wants to be your rock. He wants to sustain you. He wants you to know that He cares for you. Charles Spurgeon said that sorrow is *the cloud which brings the shower of supplication.*[1] Have you ever gone along for weeks and weeks and the extent of your prayers might have been: *Bless this. Praise the Lord. Thank You, Lord?* Then, all of a sudden, sorrow hit. You got down on your knees and prayed as you hadn't prayed in days, weeks, and months, and then you rose feeling powerful with God. Have you ever said, *Lord, let suffering do its part in my life so that it will force me to the place of prayer?* Sometimes nothing but suffering will

---

[1] Spurgeon, C. H. "A Woman of a Sorrowful Spirit." *The Metropolitan Tabernacle Pulpit* 26 (1880): 37.

bring a shower of supplication, and then it does a work in your heart to give you empathy for others who are suffering.

In a sermon called "A Woman of a Sorrowful Spirit," Spurgeon said, *If we are of a sorrowful spirit, we may... be of a prayerful spirit. ...* [2] I love that. He said something else that is so sweet: *O daughter of sorrow, if in thy darkened chamber thou shalt learn the art of prevailing with the Well-beloved, you bright-eyed maidens, adown whose cheeks no tears have ever rushed, may well envy you, for to be proficient in the art and mystery of prayer is to be as a prince with God.* [3]

So, what was the outcome of Hannah's prayer? According to I Samuel 1:12–18, it transformed her: *And it came to pass, as she continued praying before the LORD, that Eli marked her mouth. Now Hannah, she spake in her heart; only her lips moved, but her voice was not heard: therefore Eli thought she had been drunken. And Eli said unto her, How long wilt thou be drunken? put away thy wine from thee.*

And Hannah answered and said, No, my lord, I am a woman of a sorrowful spirit: I have drunk neither wine nor strong drink, but have poured out my soul before the LORD. Count not thine handmaid for a daughter of Belial: for out of the abundance of my complaint and grief have I spoken hitherto.

Then Eli answered and said, Go in peace: and the God of Israel grant thee thy petition that thou hast asked of him.

And she said, Let thine handmaid find grace in thy sight. So the woman went her way, and did eat, and her countenance was no more sad (KJV).

Hannah prayed and wept greatly, and she continued praying until she received comfort and peace. Verse 18 says she *went her way, and did eat, and her countenance was no more sad.* Nothing had really changed. She didn't bear a baby immediately. Peninnah still had children and she didn't. But she had the promise of God that He was going to work, and she believed Him. Can you do that? Faith produces prayer, and prayer produces faith. It's like a circle. Hannah came away from the

---

[2] Ibid.

[3] Ibid.

place of prayer believing. The Bible tells us her countenance was no more sad and she ate. God had worked on her behalf, but it was at least nine months before her circumstances changed.

God was faithful to His promise through Eli. In verse 27, Hannah said, *For this child I prayed; and the LORD hath given me my petition which I asked of him* (KJV). Isn't that beautiful? The Lord gave her the petition that she had asked of Him. When we go in bitterness of spirit and sorrow of heart, God is always willing to meet us and to answer. Now, He might not change those people, and He might not change those circumstances, but He'll change you. If you are changed, you can bear up under it. When you know He cares for you, and He's helping, it will give you strength and the ability to withstand the wiliest enemy.

God answered Hannah's prayer and caused her to triumph over her foe. In her prayer of praise and worship in chapter 2, verse 1, she said, *My mouth is enlarged over mine enemies. The Living Bible* renders her prayer, *Now I have an answer for my enemies, for the Lord has solved my problem.* She certainly had an answer for her enemy, Peninnah. It must have been the shock of all shocks when Hannah bore a son and then three more sons and two daughters (1 Samuel 2:21). *Provoking Peninnah* was put to silence!

God is faithful. He didn't just answer her prayer. He not only gave her the desire of her heart, He gave her *abundantly above* the desire of her heart (Ephesians 3:20). He gave her a precious son, Samuel, who served and loved God throughout his entire life. From his earliest days until he was a dying old man, Samuel never once turned back from serving the Lord. I believe he was the best judge that Israel ever had, and one of the first prophets to the nation. Out of Hannah's bitterness of spirit and the provocation of an enemy that drove her to the place of prayer came precious, precious Samuel.

Hannah's prayer of thanksgiving in the second chapter is as great as the Magnificat of Mary found in Luke 1:46–55. Oh, how Hannah knew God! I don't know if she knew Him that well before her trials, but her trials brought about a deeper knowledge of Him. In her prayer of thanksgiving, she highlighted all the wonderful blessings God had showered upon her. Take time to read it for yourself in 1 Samuel 2:1–10. God not only answered her prayer by giving her Samuel, but *the Lord visited* her (1 Samuel 2:21). We don't know in what form He visited her, but how would you like to have Jesus visit you today? I would. I'd like Him to sit down in bodily presence and talk with me for a while. I think most of us would.

There's a panorama that I want you to see that I think is so important. We do have adversaries. We do have difficult tasks. We do go through trials and testings. But, as we do, we can be assured that there is not one trial or test that isn't a part of God's divine plan. God didn't just have a plan for Hannah to bring forth Samuel; He has a plan for you as well.

We can look back on Hannah's life and see what God was doing because we have the full story. He allowed Hannah to be barren because she would be so desperate in spirit that she would be willing to bear a son and give him to God. He needed a man to judge Israel that would be a godly, faithful man. He needed a man that would be raised up under Eli in the temple all the days of his boyhood. There was nobody in all of Israel like that at that time. We can see how God, in wanting a man like Samuel, had to allow Hannah to become so desperate and bitter in soul from the provocation of her adversary that she would go to the tabernacle and vow to give God the baby that He would give unto her.

Can you see God's overall plan? God didn't let Peninnah provoke Hannah for no reason. Likewise, He has a divine purpose for us in every situation, even though it may originate from Satan or an adversary. It could be for our growth. God uses trials to cause us to come to a place of consecration that we've never come to before. He can then use us in situations where we will be effective for Him. Without those trials, we may never have been as effective. See that, realize it, and be blessed by it.

Before Chuck and I moved back to Costa Mesa from Corona, California, I thought I knew a lot about submission, and in all the major areas of our life together, I had been submissive. However, I began to struggle in this area when Chuck said, *Kay, I want to move back to Costa Mesa.*

He had been invited to become the pastor of a little church of about twenty-five people. There was fighting in the church, and all sorts of problems. We had only been living in Corona for a year. Chuck was gone all week building motel units near Idyllwild because his current pastoral position didn't pay enough to provide food, clothing, and rent. Our daughter, Jan, had gone to three high schools already; our boys, Chuck Jr. and Jeff, had transferred junior high schools; and, our daughter, Cheryl, had just started kindergarten. Because of all these issues, I didn't think it made a great deal of sense to take the position in Costa Mesa.

Additionally, I had developed a *know-it-all* spirit because God had given me the word of knowledge in many situations and with numerous people in our churches. (This is a terrible confession, but I'm baring my heart.) I thought I knew better. I thought that at that juncture in our lives, I had the mind of the Lord. I thought he was crazy, really, to move back to twenty-five people in an arguing, fighting church. I wanted to be submissive, but I didn't want to move.

For three weeks I carried on, not with words of anger, but with this grieving spirit. I couldn't stop crying. I was very worried about the people in our church in Corona. I was worried about our children and their adjustment to another school. There were many concerns on my heart. I was praying, but from the perspective of, *Oh God, please change Chuck. Please! The people here need him! And, the children shouldn't have to change schools again! Oh Lord, open his eyes to see.* I went on and on like that in my prayers.

At the end of three weeks, I still didn't feel any better and nothing about the situation had changed. Chuck was emphatic about the move and I was still begging him to abandon the idea. Finally, one day I was alone on my knees in the front room of our house with *The Living Bible* open in front of me. I cried out to the Lord, *I commit my way completely unto You. Please remove all will of my own, and all of my blindness. Change me. I am in bitterness of spirit and soul, and I don't know the answer. Please show me what to do.* In front of me, my Bible had opened to 1 Corinthians 11:3, which says, *A wife is responsible to her husband, her husband is responsible to Christ, and Christ is responsible to God* (emphasis added). I had my answer.

I wasn't responsible for the people in the church. I wasn't responsible for anything except my attitude of submission to Chuck. God blessed Hannah far, far above what she ever imagined when she came to the place of submission. He also blessed me far, far above what I could have imagined when I surrendered my will in the front room of our house in Corona.

I've thought so many times of what God has given me. Chuck and I don't have any needs except spiritual needs. Look at the church that God has blessed Chuck with—so many people! Chuck has often said he would have been content with a church of two hundred and fifty people. He thought that was the ideal church size for him to pastor well. Look what God has done instead! Day after day I'm amazed. I'm praising Him and rejoicing because He has done exceedingly abundantly above all that I could have asked or thought, and He wants to do the same thing for you! Turn your life over to Him and He'll make it *significant*, as James 4:10 in the *Amplified Bible* tells us. He'll cause you to be used in such a dynamic way that you will look back and think, *Oh, why didn't I turn my life over to Him before this?*

Are you provoked by adversaries? Are you in bitterness of soul or spirit today? Are you confused or distressed? God alone knows how to resolve your problems. He knows the problems in your marriage. He knows the physical problems that you may be going through. Perhaps you are struggling with emotional problems; you are staggering beneath a burden and are discouraged, despondent, or in despair. At this very moment, reach out to Him in prayer because He cares and is your refuge and strength, a very present help in trouble.

Reflections

1. Ponder Hannah's prayerful response to the burdens of her life.
2. What do you do with the difficulties in your life and why is prayer an absolute necessity?
3. How are prayer and faith tied together?
4. Hannah received comfort, peace, and the promise of God when she prayed. What results can you expect when you pray?
5. Bring the concerns of your heart before the Lord, believing He will keep His promise to do exceedingly, abundantly above all you can ask or think.

About the Author

Popular women's speaker and author, Kay Smith, is director of the Joyful Life Women's Ministry at Calvary Chapel Costa Mesa, California, where she has served alongside her husband of fifty-six years, Chuck Smith, senior pastor of Calvary Chapel Costa Mesa and founder of Calvary Chapel, which has over fifteen hundred affiliates worldwide. In addition to being a homemaker and helping to raise the couple's four grown children, Kay assisted Chuck during the early years in their ministry as a church pianist and secretary.

Pain and sorrow come in many varieties, but God is faithful to give us comfort by the Holy Spirit, through brothers and sisters in Christ that love and pray for us, and through the words of Scripture, which enable us to see purpose in our pain.

—Leslie Martin

Dorcas

A Woman of Service

by Leslie Martin

Older women likewise are to be reverent in their behavior, not malicious gossips nor enslaved to much wine, teaching what is good, that they may encourage the young women to love their husbands, to love their children, to be sensible, pure, workers at home, kind.

—Titus 2:3–5, NASB

One of the qualities of a godly woman is kindness or goodness (as *kindness* is translated in the *King James Version*). Proverbs 31:20 says, *She opens her arms to the poor and extends her hands to the needy* (NIV). The word *poor* here refers to those that are hurting physically. So often, Calvary sisters come alongside those who are ill by bringing them food, visiting them in the hospital, caring for their children while they go to doctor appointments, giving money, or providing for them to go to a retreat or special event. We are to open our arms to those who are hurting physically.

The *needy* are those who are hurting emotionally or spiritually. Everything may be fine economically and someone can be in the best of health, but they still have needs. They may be lonely or grieving. They may be struggling with a difficult relationship, either with children, a spouse, a family member, a co-worker, or a friend, and they need someone to stretch out their hand and encourage them. They may be hurting spiritually. Perhaps they haven't come to know Jesus Christ, and they are spiritually dead. The younger woman is to be taught and trained by older, godly women how to be kind to those who are hurting physically, emotionally, or spiritually.

There's a beautiful example in the New Testament of a godly woman who put kindness into practice. She literally opened her arms to the poor and stretched out her hands to the needy. Her story is recorded in Acts 9:36–42: *Now in Joppa there was a disciple named Tabitha (which translated in Greek is called Dorcas); this woman was abounding with deeds of kindness and charity which she continually did. And it happened at that time that she fell sick and died; and when they had washed her body, they laid it in an upper room. Since Lydda was near Joppa, the disciples, having heard that Peter was there, sent two men to him, imploring him, "Do not delay in coming to us." So Peter arose and went with them. When he arrived, they brought him into the upper room; and all the widows stood beside him, weeping and showing all the tunics and garments that Dorcas used to make while she was with them. But Peter sent them all out and knelt down and prayed, and turning to the body, he said, "Tabitha, arise." And she opened her eyes, and when she saw Peter, she sat up. And he gave her his hand and raised her up; and calling the saints and widows, he presented her alive. It became known all over Joppa, and many believed in the Lord* (NASB).

Dorcas was a godly woman who showed kindness by using her hands to bless others. She lived in the seaport town of Joppa, which is located on the Mediterranean Sea about thirty miles west of Jerusalem. It is an ancient city that still exists and is presently known as Jaffa. The apostle Peter once stayed about ten miles from Joppa in the town of Lydda, which was located on the route to Jerusalem.

It isn't recorded that Jesus ever went to Joppa. We know Dorcas was one of His Jewish disciples, so perhaps she had seen or heard Him during one of the three yearly feasts when the Jews gathered at the Temple in Jerusalem. We also know that Dorcas was one of only seven persons recorded in Scripture to have been raised from the dead, and that she was the only adult woman in that group.

Fishing was the main occupation in Joppa. Scholars are sure that Joppa had a high proportion of widows because this occupation was so dangerous, especially at that time when sudden storms and unexplained weather would have been particularly hazardous to ancient boats. We don't know whether or not Dorcas was a widow, but it is likely since Scripture doesn't mention that she was married and because her ministry focus was helping widows. When you've gone through suffering yourself, it opens your heart to help others who are experiencing the same kind of pain. Perhaps, because of what she had gone through as a widow, Dorcas wanted to show kindness towards others going through the same thing.

Second Corinthians 1:3–4 says, *Blessed be the God and Father of our Lord Jesus Christ, the Father of mercies and God of all comfort, who comforts us in all our affliction so that we will be able to comfort those who are in any affliction with the comfort with which we ourselves are comforted by God* (NASB). God, in His great mercy, allows us to go through suffering, not because He delights in our pain, but because He delights in receiving glory. He is magnified when the life of Christ shines through us. First Corinthians 10:13 says, *No temptation* [or trial, or testing] *has overtaken you but such as is common to man; and God is faithful, who will not allow you to be tempted beyond what you are able, but with the temptation* [or testing, or trial] *will provide the way of escape also, so that you will be able to endure it.*

The Lord has blessed my husband, Mark, and me with so much encouragement during times of suffering as people have told us they love us and are praying for us. The Scripture also provides great comfort. One time as Mark was going through an episode of kidney stones, he read a verse in the Psalms about suffering. He looked up the word that was translated *suffering* in the passage and discovered that it meant "a stone in a narrow place." He thought, *That describes my suffering exactly. My kidney stone is in this narrow, little place.* Yet the promise was that God would be with him and would bring him through. He was comforted and encouraged through the Scripture.

Everyone has gone through difficult times in life—perhaps through the loss of a child, physical or emotional suffering, or a relationship that brings sorrow, loneliness, grief, or even spiritual suffering. Pain and sorrow come in many varieties, but God is faithful to give us comfort by the Holy Spirit, through brothers and sisters in Christ that love and pray for us, and through the words of Scripture, which enable us to see purpose in our pain.

One of the Scriptures that God has often used to comfort and encourage me is Lamentations 3:22–23: *Through the LORD's mercies we are not consumed, because His compassions fail not. They are new every morning; great is Your faithfulness.* Many times when I have gone to bed at night hurting and not able to move because of rheumatoid arthritis, this Scripture has come to my mind. The Lord has spoken to my heart as I laid my head on my pillow exhausted, not feeling well, and without another ounce of strength for that day. He has reminded me that in the morning, He will give new mercy, new strength, and new grace for another day. I can rejoice knowing that my Savior is there, ready and willing to give me what I need. Every morning there are new mercies from Him.

I have often used that Scripture to encourage other people. Their pain may be emotional. Perhaps they've lost a loved one and they think, *Every morning I wake up and every night I go to bed, and I just don't know if I'll be able to live one more day. I miss them so much. I'm so lonely, so lost, so overwhelmed with grief.* And yet, God's promise is that every morning He'll give new grace for that day. We can continue another twenty-four hours because the Lord will be our strength. God gives us comfort in the things that we go through, not just to comfort us, but to equip us to comfort others.

Perhaps someone has tried to comfort you and it has not been very comforting. When trying to encourage or comfort someone who is going through the loss of a spouse or is suffering a terrible trial, there are some statements that hurt more than they help.

For example, don't say, *I know exactly how you feel.* Even if you have gone through something similar, you don't know exactly how the person feels. Jesus Christ knows how they feel. He is our merciful and faithful High Priest who has compassion on us, and who suffered in all points as we suffer, yet without sin (Hebrews 4:15). None of us knows another person as well as the Lord knows him or her. The first thing a person thinks when you say those words is, *No, you don't.* It brings out self-justification and defensiveness. It is better to say, *I don't know exactly how you are feeling, but I've gone through something similar, and I know it was difficult. Can I put my arm around you and listen, or just sit with you and be quiet?* Let them know you care.

If someone dies, don't say, *Maybe Jesus needed your loved one more than you do.* Those words are not comforting. Jesus doesn't take people home to heaven because He needs them. He has close fellowship with us here on earth. When you say something like that, it creates a conflict between the grieving person and Jesus and may cause them to feel angry toward the Lord. Even a mature believer might have difficulty with that statement.

Another misstatement is, *If so-and-so had lived, some terrible catastrophe would have happened to them.* When my three-year-old nephew, Carl, drowned in a bathtub after what we think was a seizure, a couple of people said, *You can praise God that he died and went to be with the Lord because if he had lived, he would have been a vegetable.* If God had allowed him to live, He would have given grace for the situation, or He could have healed him. But God, in His grace and in His awesome foreknowledge, omnipotence, and omniscience knew what was best for Carl.

What is helpful for ministering to someone in pain? Isaiah 50:4 says, *The Lord GOD has given Me the tongue of disciples, that I may know how to sustain the weary one with a word. He awakens Me morning by morning, He awakens My ear to listen as a disciple* (NASB). First, it is helpful to seek the Lord about how to comfort a needy person. You may read a Scripture in your quiet time that seems encouraging but doesn't apply to a current situation in your own life. Later, the Lord may bring that Scripture to mind for someone else because He wants you to use it to encourage them.

This happened to me recently. I'd had a really bad day and was upset about what Mark and I were going through. I was reveling in fleshly thinking: *I'm sick of this. I've had enough. I want out!* A precious sister walked up to me after church and said, *The Lord gave me this Scripture during my quiet time about a week ago and I really thought it was for you but haven't had a chance to tell you. The Scripture said, "Be faithful unto death, and I will give you the crown of life"* (Revelation 2:10, NASB). She wasn't struggling with faithfulness in her own life, but I was that day and the Lord prompted her to speak to me at the exact time that I needed to hear those words. I was so blessed and comforted.

Second, Romans 12:15 says, *Rejoice with those who rejoice, and weep with those who weep* (NASB). It is helpful to identify with the person's suffering and grief. Don't pity them or try to make them happy, just share in their sorrow. The Scripture says we should be so intimately tied to our brothers and sisters in Christ that we praise God with them when they are blessed and empathize with them when they are sorrowful.

My little nephew, Carl, died on a Saturday night. When we got the news, we drove to Tucson, Arizona, and were there just after he had gone to be with the Lord. It was a very rough night, but we drove back for the Sunday morning services. What a comfort it was to have brothers and sisters in Christ come up to us and cry with us and hug us. They didn't try to give great theological reasons as to why this tragedy happened, they didn't try to explain it away, and they didn't say, *I know exactly how you feel; this is what you need to do.* They just cried with us, and it was comforting.

Third, Psalm 119:28 says, *My soul weeps because of grief; strengthen me according to Your word* (NASB). And then verse 50 says, *This is my comfort in my affliction, that Your word has revived me.* God's words are perfect words. They are inspired by the Holy Spirit and they will touch the heart. It is much more comforting to receive encouragement from God's Word than from our own opinions, feelings, thoughts, and reasoning. It is much better to strengthen someone with the Word of God.

Finally, when you want to encourage and comfort someone, don't stay away from them. Remember them. Sometimes we're really good about ministering to people when they're right in the middle of the crisis, but then we forget about them a week, a month, a year later, or at important times in their lives. An illustration of this is when someone has experienced the death of a close loved one. Everyone is there at the funeral and for a week or two later, sending cards, making meals, calling, or stopping by to console the person. But what about six months later when their loved one's birthday comes up? Or, at holiday times like Christmas, Thanksgiving, or anniversaries? Those are important times, too. True comfort is offered not just in the emergency room, but over the long haul. We should be there for the rehab sessions—the physical, emotional, and spiritual therapy, so to speak. Don't stay away from those who are suffering. Remember them. It doesn't take much. Just be available to listen, give a hug, or help out.

All of us can be used to comfort someone else. Use whatever God has given you. What do you have in your hand? Think of a man like Moses. He had a shepherd's staff in his hand when God called him. Yet, God used it as the means of deliverance for the Jews. David had a slingshot and a harp. God used the things that were accessible to work through his life and bless other people. Think about the slingshot. God used that simple little child's toy or shepherd's weapon to fell the mighty giant Goliath and save the people of Israel. Ruth only had an apron, but she went to the fields of Boaz, gleaned grain, and put it in her apron. She used what she had to help and bless her mother-in-law, Naomi. Miriam was a prophetess who spoke forth for the Lord many times. She had a tambourine in her hand, and when the children of Israel were delivered through the Red Sea, Miriam grabbed her tambourine and led the women of Israel in praise and worship to the Lord.

Dorcas used her sewing needle, her thread, and her fabric to make clothing for widows and their children. Her goal in life was to encourage and comfort others. What a beautiful mission in life. May the Lord instill that mission in each one of us. Titus 2:5 commands the older women to teach the younger women to be good or kind. Dorcas had been taught and trained as a disciple to be kind and her life was an example of the godly woman who does good.

James 1:27 says that our religion is shown, not by what we say, but by what we do: *Pure and undefiled religion in the sight of our God and Father is this: to visit orphans and widows in their distress, and to keep oneself unstained by the world* (NASB). True religion is caring for those who are in need. It's getting our hands in to help.

Dorcas was a Jewish believer in Jesus Christ, and Judaism is characterized by doing good deeds. The study of the Word and the Torah are very important, as is the declaration of *Sh'ma Yisrael Adonai Elohaynu Adonai Echad*, which is translated *Hear, O Israel! The* LORD *is our God, the* LORD *is one!* (Deuteronomy 6:4, NASB) But even more important are the actions, good deeds, and *mitzvahs* that a person does. Because of her background, Dorcas had been trained her entire life that it was important not just to say good things, but to do good.

Deuteronomy 14:27–29 says, *You shall not neglect the Levite who is in your town, for he has no portion or inheritance among you. At the end of every third year you shall bring out all the tithe of your produce in that year, and shall deposit it in your town. The Levite, because he has no portion or inheritance among you, and the alien* [foreign resident], *the orphan and the widow who are in your town, shall come and eat and be satisfied, in order that the* LORD *your God may bless you in all the work of your hand which you do* (NASB).

When the land was divided, the tribe of Levi was not given a portion, so every other tribe was required to provide for the Levites. Every three years, 10 percent of what was grown, raised, or earned in that year was deposited in a common treasury in each town, not only for the Levites, but also for the widows, aliens, and orphans. In order to receive the blessing of God under the old covenant, a person was required to contribute to this offering that acted as a social security system. As a Jew, Dorcas was trained to care for the poor and needy. Every third year of her adult life, she would have given 10 percent of what she earned for this purpose.

In Exodus 22:22–24 the Lord says, *You shall not afflict any widow or fatherless child. If you afflict them in any way, and they cry at all to*

Me, I will surely hear their cry, and My wrath will become hot, and I will kill you with the sword, and your wives shall be widows, and your children fatherless. God took His people's responsibility to care for the widows and orphans seriously. If they mistreated, ignored, or did not provide for those who were suffering, God would hear their cry and come to their defense.

Similarly, Deuteronomy 10:17–18 says, *The LORD your God is the God of gods and the Lord of lords, the great, the mighty, and the awesome God who does not show partiality, nor take a bribe. He executes justice for the orphan and the widow, and shows His love for the alien by giving him food and clothing* (NASB). God will take up the cause of the orphan and widow to make sure they get justice. He shows His love by providing their food and clothing.

Deuteronomy 24:17 says, *You shall not pervert the justice due an alien or an orphan, nor take a widow's garment in pledge* (NASB). In Old Testament times (and even today), there were people so perverse that they would show no compassion towards a widow. They would require her to repay a debt even if she hadn't personally incurred the debt. It might have been left by her husband when he died. God said the widow was not to be reduced to the point of not having clothing or food; her coat was not to be taken in pledge to be held until she was able to repay what was owed.

Deuteronomy 24:19–22 commands, *When you reap your harvest in your field and have forgotten a sheaf in the field, you shall not go back to get it; it shall be for the alien, for the orphan, and for the widow, in order that the LORD your God may bless you in all the work of your hands. When you beat your olive tree, you shall not go over the boughs again; it shall be for the alien, for the orphan, and for the widow. When you gather the grapes of your vineyard, you shall not go over it again; it shall be for the alien, for the orphan, for the widow. And you shall remember that you were a slave in the land of Egypt; therefore I am commanding you to do this thing* (NASB).

If someone had a vineyard, an olive tree, or a field that had been planted, they were not to harvest every bit of produce. The owner was allowed to go through it once, and then the gleanings (whatever was left after harvest) would be available for the widows and orphans to gather. The purpose was to remind people of their former hardships. They had been slaves in Egypt, but God delivered them and blessed them; now they were to share that blessing with others who were going through difficult times in their lives.

Leviticus 23:22 says that not only were the gleanings to be left for the widows and orphans, but the fields were not to be stripped bare during the first harvest. Growers were permitted to collect most of the bounty from a field of grain or barley, but all four corners of the field were to be left untouched so the poor could gather both from what the harvesters had missed and from the un-harvested portions of the field.

This system can be seen in a familiar story in the book of Ruth. Ruth and her mother-in-law, Naomi, were both widows, and Ruth was an alien from Moab. They returned to Bethlehem from Moab after their husbands had died, and Ruth gleaned in the fields of a righteous man named Boaz. He not only allowed her to glean what was left over after his men had gone through the field and from the untouched corners of the field, but he also instructed them to drop grain on the ground so that she would have more to gather. This was how God provided for the widows and orphans. We can assume that one reason Dorcas had a heart to help the widows was because she had been taught that God cares about the needy. He wants us to care about the needy as well.

Acts 9:36 says, *Now in Joppa there was a certain disciple named Tabitha* (NASB). Dorcas is the only woman in the New Testament to be given the title *disciple*. The word *disciple* means "follower," and Dorcas followed the Lord's example as His disciple. How did she do this? Jesus described the call of His ministry when He claimed to be the fulfillment of Isaiah 61:1–2, which says, *The Spirit of the Lord GOD is upon Me, because the LORD has anointed Me to preach good tidings to the poor; He has sent Me to heal the brokenhearted, to proclaim liberty to the captives, and the opening of the prison to those who are bound; to proclaim the acceptable year of the LORD.*

Jesus was sent to bind up the brokenhearted; and much of His ministry was involved in healing the sick, raising the dead, cleansing the lepers, giving sight to the blind, hearing to the deaf, speech to those who could not speak, and the ability to walk to those who could not walk. As a disciple of the Lord, Dorcas followed in her Lord's footsteps, doing those things that would bind up the brokenhearted. She simply took her needle and thread and provided clothing for those in need.

Matthew 10:24–25 says, *A disciple is not above his teacher, nor a slave above his master. It is enough for the disciple that he become as his teacher, and the slave as his master* (NASB). A disciple of Jesus is somebody who not only follows the Lord and His example, but wants to become like Jesus, and is allowing the Holy Spirit to transform her into the likeness of Jesus Christ. Scripture says that now we see through a glass darkly, but then we will see face to face (1 Corinthians 13:12). Someday we shall be like Jesus because we shall see Him as He is (1 John 3:2). Even here on earth, the Lord, through His Spirit, is at work in us to will and to do His good pleasure (Philippians 2:13). He is making us more and more like Jesus Christ. One of the prayers I pray almost daily is that my children would grow as Jesus grew when He was on earth. Scripture says He grew in wisdom, in stature, and in favor with God and men (Luke 2:52). I want my kids to be disciples of the Lord, not only following the Lord, but becoming like Him.

Jesus was a man of sorrows and acquainted with grief (Isaiah 53:3), and Dorcas was acquainted with grief—if not her own, then that of the widows to whom she ministered. She accepted what the Lord allowed in her life and used it to reach out to others in love. Instead of asking why: *Why is this happening to me? Why has my husband died? Why am I going through such a hard time in life?*— she asked what: *What will You have me to do? What is Your purpose for my life?* It is so easy to get caught up in the *whys*: *Why am I sick? Why does my friend treat me with indifference? Why didn't my children call me on Mother's Day? Why, why, why?* All that does is create more questions, more hurt, and more suffering. Instead of asking why, ask what: *What can I gain from this experience? What can I learn that will comfort and help others? What do You want me to do?* Dorcas didn't ask why. She asked what.

Luke 14:25–27 says, *Now large crowds were going along with Him; and He turned and said to them, "If anyone comes to Me, and does not hate his own father and mother and wife and children and brothers and sisters, yes, and even his own life, he cannot be My disciple. Whoever does not carry his own cross and come after Me cannot be My disciple"* (NASB).

It is important to understand what the Scripture means when it uses the word *hate* in this context. When Jesus says that if you don't hate all earthly relationships, then you can't be His disciple, He is not saying that you are to despise your father and mother. He is making a contrast. You are to love Jesus more than everyone else, and your love for Him should be so great that, comparatively, it will be as if you hate everyone else. Jesus was Dorcas' first love, her supreme love, and her only love; all other loves paled in comparison. She lived for Jesus above anything or anyone else.

In John 13:34–35 Jesus said, *A new commandment I give to you, that you love one another, even as I have loved you, that you also love one another. By this all men will know that you are My disciples, if you have love for one another* (NASB). Dorcas' love was evidence that she was a disciple of Jesus. Her life was devoted to helping those that were on the heart of God. We are to love as Jesus loved. We are to love those who can't give anything in return, as Dorcas loved the widows and orphans.

In 1 Corinthians 13, the beautiful chapter that speaks of love, the apostle Paul tells us that we may speak God's truth with eloquence and even use heavenly language, but if we don't have love, we are noisy gongs or clanging cymbals. And if we know all mysteries, have all knowledge, and have faith to remove mountains but we don't have love, we are nothing. And if we give all our possessions to feed the poor and deliver our bodies to be burned, but don't have love, it profits us nothing.

Love is the key. We can say good things and even do good things, but it takes the love of Jesus Christ blowing through our lives to truly make any of our words or actions a blessing to others. Dorcas was a godly woman who was trained and taught by the Spirit of God to be kind. We older women are to encourage and train younger women. If you are a younger woman, you are to be encouraged and trained in how to be kind, loving, and good in helping others—not just by what we say, but by what we do to bless our brothers and sisters in Christ.

Reflections

1. Stop and consider the servant heart of Dorcas.
2. How did her works prove the genuineness of her faith?
3. In what ways do your works give evidence of your faith and love for others?

4. What resources (gifts, talents, material assets) can you devote to the work of the kingdom? Be specific.

5. Take a moment to prayerfully place these things at His disposal and ask Him to enable you to serve Him more fully.

About the Author

Leslie Martin is the wife of Senior Pastor Mark Martin of Calvary Community Church in Phoenix, Arizona. She is the director of Calvary's Heart & Home Women's Ministry and also teaches three women's Bible studies each week. Her teaching ministry is broadcast through the *New Mercies* radio program. She is a home-schooling mother of three terrific children: Emily (15), Ellie (13), and Daniel (10).

The most important thing we can do
as women is to point people to Jesus and
encourage them in their walk with the
Lord.

—Cheryl Cahill

Deborah

A Woman of War

by Cheryl Cahill

---

*Then Deborah said to Barak, "Up! For this is the day in which
the LORD has delivered Sisera into your hand. Has not the LORD
gone out before you?"*
—Judges 4:14

Twelve ordinary men and one woman ruled Israel after Joshua
died. These judges were imperfect, but they became heroes because
they were submissive to God. The book of Judges tells their story,
but it is also a book about sin and its consequences. Although the
book ends on a note of victory—with the nation taking a stand for
God and ready to experience His blessings—there was a leadership
vacuum after the death of Joshua, and the nation was left without
a strong central government. Instead of enjoying freedom and
prosperity in the Promised Land, Israel entered into the Dark Ages
of its history. The people lost both their spiritual commitment and
their motivation; apathy began to set in.

Sometimes the first step away from God is incomplete obedience. Partial obedience is still disobedience. Judges 1 tells us that
even though God had directed them to completely eliminate their
enemies from the land, the Israelites refused. They compromised
by intermarrying with the Canaanites and by worshipping idols. By

the end of the reign of the judges, everyone was doing what was right in their own eyes (much like today when some Christians worship the gods of money, prosperity, and materialism).

Before long, the people were taken captive by other nations and would beg God to rescue them. In faithfulness to His promise and out of His lovingkindness, God would raise up a judge to deliver them. For a time there would be peace. However, complacency and disobedience would set in once again, and this cycle would repeat itself. In times of prosperity, the people didn't think they needed God. They would start to trust in self, and then wander away from Him. God would often use Israel's enemies to draw them back to Himself, just as He uses a variety of trials to lead His people back into freedom and true worship today. Refusing to learn from the past, the Israelites kept making the same mistake of living only for the moment. Their recurring spiral downward into sin is evident throughout the book of Judges. Conversely, God's mercy and love shine forth continually as He repeatedly delivered them from bondage.

In Judges 4, we see how God intervened on behalf of Israel by providing spiritual leadership through a judge named Deborah. Her name means "bee," which reminds me of the familiar phrase, "busy bee." She was undoubtedly an industrious woman, given that she was the only female judge to rule Israel. She wasn't too busy, however, to put God first in her life. She was a woman who had her priorities in order.

In Judges 4:1–3 we read, *When Ehud was dead, the children of Israel again did evil in the sight of the LORD. So the LORD sold them into the hand of Jabin king of Canaan, who reigned in Hazor. The commander of his army was Sisera, who dwelt in Harosheth Hagoyim. And the children of Israel cried out to the LORD; for Jabin had nine hundred chariots of iron, and for twenty years he had harshly oppressed the children of Israel.*

For eighty years, the Jews had enjoyed rest under Ehud's leadership, but as soon as this godly judge was dead, they once again became ensnared by the sin of idolatry. They forsook the Lord and did evil in His sight (Judges 2–3). God sent Israel's enemy, Jabin, the king of Hazor (also called the king of Canaan) as His instrument to bring about repentance and restoration for the nation. God had allowed Jabin to oppress the Israelites in the land of Canaan for twenty years. Jabin commanded a large army, which included nine hundred iron chariots with razor-like extensions projecting from the wheels. As these chariots flew across the land, the razors would spin and mow down the enemy. Can you imagine going out to war against a foe like that? No wonder the Israelites were afraid! They didn't even have horses and chariots; they were foot soldiers.

The nation of Israel had forsaken God and He would no longer help them drive the remaining Canaanites out of the land. God, in His faithfulness and patience, had repeatedly warned them. The false gods that they thought were so wonderful had actually become a snare to them, and they had only themselves to blame for the state they were in. With their lips they would promise to serve and obey God, but their hearts were far from Him, and they would bow down in the dust before Baal. Their walk didn't line up with their talk. We are not much different because we say, *Lord I want to be like You. I want to be obedient. Help me to live for You. I want to be used for Your glory.* We then waste time seeking after the lusts of our flesh and we forget the Lord, becoming self-sufficient. Sometimes we end up in an apathetic backslidden state and lose the fire in our hearts. When God withdrew His protection, the Israelites became powerless against their enemies. Life became unbearable as a result of their own sin. Their peace disappeared. When we are in sin, or get too close to the edge of temptation, we lose the peace we normally have when we are walking in right relationship with Him.

The Israelites soon forgot what it meant to be free. They were held in the iron clutches of Jabin and Sisera, the captain of the king's army. This stiff-necked people lived in fear and had no earthly place to look for deliverance. They could only look up. Have you ever found yourself in that place? You get so low and broken that you have no place to look but up. That is the best place to be because God can do the most when we are in this situation. Very often the battles we face are spiritual and God wants to show Himself mighty and powerful to deliver us. This story reminds us that *the weapons of our warfare are not carnal but mighty in God for pulling down strongholds* (2 Corinthians 10:4).

Once again, the Israelites cried out to God and He heard them. What a patient, gracious, and merciful God He is! It amazes me that we can repeatedly rebel, yet He always hears us and wants to bring us back to Himself. In this situation, He was faithful to the promise He had made generations earlier to Abraham that He would make Abraham's descendants a mighty and blessed people. God heard the cries of His people and provided a deliverer in Deborah.

Judges 4:4 says, *Now Deborah, a prophetess, the wife of Lapidoth, was judging Israel at that time.* Numbers 12:6 describes a prophet's role: *If there is a prophet among you, I, the LORD, make Myself known to him in a vision; I speak to him in a dream.* Today, God speaks to us primarily through His Word. When we read our Bibles, something seems to jump off the page and we know God is speaking specifically to us. Back then, He spoke to the prophets through visions and dreams.

God chose Deborah as a judge and prophetess, and she became well-known throughout Israel. What an honor that God would choose a woman. In those days, women were not highly esteemed, but were subject to the limitations of a male-dominated society. I think God was, in part, using this ordinary woman to humble Israel. The fact that He chose Deborah to lead the nation reminds us that we can't put God in a box. He is sovereign and can do as He chooses. His ways are not always our ways.

Verse 5 says, *And she would sit under the palm tree of Deborah between Ramah and Bethel in the mountains of Ephraim. And the children of Israel came up to her for judgment.* Picture her sitting under this beautiful palm tree meditating on the Lord. As people came and poured their hearts out to her, Deborah provided them with godly wisdom, knowledge, instruction, and encouragement in their struggles. In the midst of functioning in the role of judge and prophetess, she was called upon to bring deliverance to God's people. What an awesome privilege. God used her mightily because she was a woman who walked closely with Him in love and submission. The most important thing we can do as women is to point people to Jesus and encourage them in their walk with the Lord. We can encourage our friends, family, and children to spend time in God's Word, to trust and obey God, and then to step out in faith.

Deborah was appointed by God to bring the people back to Him and set them free from the power of the enemy. She knew that the time for liberation had come. In verses 6–7 we read, *Then she sent and called for Barak the son of Abinoam from Kedesh in Naphtali, and said to him, "Has not the LORD God of Israel commanded, 'Go and deploy troops at Mount Tabor; take with you ten thousand men of the sons of Naphtali and of the sons of Zebulun; and against you I will deploy Sisera, the commander of Jabin's army, with his chariots and his multitude at the River Kishon; and I will deliver him into your hand'?"* She gave the orders and assured Barak that he would be victorious because God had promised to deliver the enemy into his hands.

I love what Barak said to Deborah in verse 8: *If you will go with me, then I will go; but if you will not go with me, I will not go!* This big, strong guy was afraid to go out to battle. I don't blame him because the battlefield is a scary place—especially facing those chariots—and it doesn't matter whether you're a man or a woman. Barak's statement reminds me of someone else who was afraid. Exodus 3 tells us that Moses was hesitant to step out in faith and speak for God because he stuttered. Gideon was also afraid to go out to battle. He hesitated because the odds were stacked against him and God kept reducing the size of his army instead of adding to it. The common denominator for each of these leaders was God's strength made perfect in human weakness.

Perhaps He's calling you to step out in faith in a certain area in your life, but you're being held captive by that vice-grip of the Enemy—fear. You know that you can't accomplish the task at hand. Remember that He gets the glory when you step out in faith in spite of your weakness. He wants you to know and experience the promise that you can do all things through Christ who strengthens you. The result will be that He will work in you and through you.

Barak's humanity is revealed in his request. Like us, he wanted someone to go with him. Have you ever done that? Someone asks you to share the gospel with a friend in the hospital and you say, *I don't want to go alone, but I'll go if you go with me. You pray and I'll talk to them.* Barak wanted Deborah to go with him because he wanted assurance that the presence of God would be with him in the battle. In Deuteronomy 31:6, Moses said, *Be strong and of good courage, do not fear nor be afraid of them; for the LORD your God, He is the One who goes with you. He will not leave you nor forsake you.* The promise to every one of us is that when we step out in faith and obedience, God goes with us. He will never forsake us. We may wander from God, but He never leaves us.

I can relate to Barak so much because I was trembling in my boots when God called my husband and me into ministry. I was okay with having a home Bible study. That was comfortable, kind of like playing church with a small group of people. Although it seemed like a big deal at the time, there wasn't a big cost or commitment, and we weren't being called to step out into the Jordan River where we could get swept away.

Then the study started to grow and God called us to step out in faith and begin meeting on Sundays. That was a huge step. God was really asking us to take a risk. When I look back, I can see that He was stretching me. At the time, I thought He was killing me, but He was only stretching me. I've learned that God isn't satisfied to let us remain in our safe, little places, but is always calling us to move forward. He doesn't want us to huddle together in our comfort zone. He wants to use us and be glorified in us. God seems to get the most glory when we are at our weakest point because that's when people look at us and say, *No way*. With the Lord, all things are possible. Whenever He calls us to do something, He will equip us to do it. He doesn't leave us hanging, but gives us what we need as we step out in faith.

I could have protested that I was too afraid when God called us to meet on Sunday mornings. I had a whole list of reasons why we shouldn't start a church. God is a gentleman. He doesn't force His will upon us; He gives us a choice and we can say no to Him. God doesn't need us, and we are not doing Him a favor by serving Him. Sometimes it's easy to get that attitude in ministry, but in reality, it is a privilege that God would even allow us to be a part of the work He is doing in the world.

When my kids were little, they'd want to help me bake cookies and I would think, *Oh, I just want to get this done*. I knew that if the kids helped, they would eat the chocolate chips and the cookies wouldn't taste as good. When I would let them help, it would make them completely happy and they'd be so excited when their dad got home. They would race for the door, yelling, *Daddy! Daddy! Look what we made for you.*

It's like that with the Lord. He doesn't need our help, but He loves us and wants to bless us by letting us serve Him. However, God's plan doesn't get stopped when we say no. He just chooses a different instrument and blesses someone else. He had a plan for Calvary Chapel Boston, and if we had said no, we would have missed out and He would have accomplished His will through someone else.

He understands our fears and inadequacies because He knows everything about us. He wants to stretch our faith, and He is glorified in our weakness. This is what encourages others to go on. When they see us in our flesh, in our fears, and in our weakness, and then we step out in faith, they think, *If she can do that, I can too because I'm just like her.*

God brings us from strength to strength. When Rosemary Gallatin, of Calvary Chapel of Finger Lakes, New York, asked me to speak at her women's retreat, I cried. She laughed at me because I said, *You have no idea what you are asking! I am petrified, but I'm in a no-win situation. If I don't speak, I feel like I'm letting you and God down, but if I do, you're going to wish I hadn't.* She thought it was so funny and just kept laughing. She's always done that to me. When we started our church, she was there watching as I trembled in my boots, but she's seen God's faithfulness and knows I've seen God's faithfulness. She said, *Just pray about the retreat.* Barak was called to do something really frightening, and he asked Deborah to go with him because he wanted the presence of the Lord. I felt like God was telling me, *I will go with you to the retreat. Don't worry; just go.*

God saw that Barak was fearful and needed assurance of His presence as he stepped out in faith. The problem was that Barak was initially walking by sight. He saw a vast army with all those chariots. His focus was on the enemy. But in 2 Chronicles 20:15–17, God made a promise to Jehoshaphat when he was facing an enemy, saying, *Listen, all you of Judah and you inhabitants of Jerusalem, and you, King Jehoshaphat! Thus says the LORD to you: "Do not be afraid nor dismayed because of this great multitude, for the battle is not yours, but God's. Tomorrow go down against them. They will surely come up by the Ascent of Ziz, and you will find them at the end of the brook before the Wilderness of Jeruel. You will not need to fight in this battle. Position yourselves, stand still and see the salvation of the LORD, who is with you, O Judah and Jerusalem!" Do not fear or be dismayed; tomorrow go out against them, for the LORD is with you.* I love that. God uses ordinary people, but He goes with them to help.

In Numbers chapter 13, we read that representatives from each of the tribes of Israel were sent to spy out the Promised Land flowing with milk and honey. They returned with reports about terrifying giants, saying, *We are grasshoppers in their sight; there is no way we can stand up against them* (see verse 33). We often do the same thing. God calls us to step out, and we get dismayed and discouraged by looking at the giants. Unbelief sets in and we say, *I can't do this. I'm too weak. I'm a grasshopper.* As long as we have that mindset, we will be unable to enter into the Promised Land, which is a type of the life of victory.

We will also never learn to fight giants if we don't step out in faith. God doesn't want us to walk by sight because from our view we only see the hindrances. This story shows us that things appear very differently to God. From His perspective, Israel's enemy was already defeated. The Canaanite army and its deadly chariots were nothing in God's sight. He wanted Barak to step out in faith and fight, and He wants the same from us. Barak accepted the challenge, and by asking Deborah to go with him, he acknowledged her as his superior in faith and courage, and God honored that.

In Judges 4:9, Deborah said, *I will surely go with you; nevertheless there will be no glory for you in the journey you are taking, for the LORD will sell Sisera into the hand of a woman.* In permitting Deborah to go, God took the honor from the men and gave it to the women, but Barak didn't seem to care about honor. He only wanted assurance of the presence of God. He took a risk and trusted God's promise, and the enemy was overtaken. In verses 14–15 we read, *Deborah said to Barak, "Up! For this is the day in which the LORD has delivered Sisera into your hand. Has not the LORD gone out before you?" So Barak went down from Mount Tabor with ten thousand men following him. And the LORD routed Sisera and all his chariots and all his army with the edge of the sword before Barak; and Sisera alighted from his chariot and fled away on foot.*

We serve a supernatural God. From Barak's point of view, things looked pretty bad. He was faced with a mighty army of men who were ready and willing to fight. But chapter 5 tells us that God sent a tremendous rainstorm that caused the Kishon River to overflow. This was an amazing occurrence because it was the dry season. The soldiers would never have expected rain during that particular time so they were unprepared when the battlefield turned to mud and the chariots and horses got stuck. What a sight it must have been! Israel's army was able to sweep in and wipe out this fierce enemy. I love what it says in verse 15: God routed the men. That means God sent confusion into the minds of the enemy. Their weapons were no match for God.

Verses 17–20 tell us that Sisera ran for his life. He was exhausted from the battle so he sought refuge in Jael's tent. She served him warm milk and tucked him into bed, making him feel so safe, protected, and comfy-cozy that he fell asleep. In verse 21, we see Deborah's prophecy fulfilled: *Then Jael, Heber's wife, took a tent peg and took a hammer in her hand, and went softly to him and drove the peg into his temple, and it went down into the ground; for he was fast asleep and weary. So he died.* God really has a sense of humor. Of course he died! The tent peg went right through his head and into the ground. This guy was literally nailed!

Was Jael's action justified? She was deceitful and she killed a defenseless man who had trusted her and was under her protection. In chapter 5, Deborah sings Jael's praises. God used her to complete His plan for His people. Sometimes we don't fully understand why God does what He does, or why He uses certain people. We can ask Him about it when we get to heaven, but we can be sure that God is sovereign and that He judges wickedness.

Verse 23 describes the victory: *So on that day God subdued Jabin king of Canaan in the presence of the children of Israel. And the hand of the children of Israel grew stronger and stronger against Jabin king of Canaan, until they had destroyed Jabin king of Canaan.* God used many people to accomplish His plan, but ultimately He received the glory because He was the one who put an end to the enemy and brought the victory.

Deborah and Barak's song of praise and thanksgiving in Judges chapter 5 is very famous. It puts everything into perspective and shows us that God, once again, proved Himself faithful to His people and to His covenant. Their faith was strengthened and they were on fire once again. In verses 2 and 9, Deborah and Barak offer their gratitude to the people who were willing to fight alongside them, saying that these brave men were serious about fighting the Lord's battles.

Alternately, in verses 15–18, they sang, *Among the divisions of Reuben there were great resolves of heart. Why did you sit among the sheepfolds, to hear the pipings for the flocks? The divisions of Reuben have great searchings of heart. Gilead stayed beyond the Jordan, and why did Dan remain on ships?*

Asher continued at the seashore, and stayed by his inlets. Zebulun is a people who jeopardized their lives to the point of death, Naphtali also, on the heights of the battlefield. This really caught my attention because it is a description of the tribes that stayed home instead of going into battle. It says they had regrets and uneasy consciences because they didn't want to leave their comfort zone. They never got to experience the victory.

As I read this, I was reminded of the words spoken by Reuben, Gad, and the half-tribe of Manasseh in Numbers 32:5. Not much had changed with some of these people. They were the ones that didn't want to cross over into the Promised Land after forty years of wandering in the wilderness. They were willing to help their fellow Jews defeat the inhabitants of the land, but they didn't want to dwell there. They had many possessions and wanted to stay where it was comfortable and safe. They told Moses they needed to build sheepfolds and get their families and flocks settled on the east side of the Jordan River before they crossed over to help their brethren fight. Essentially, they said, *We'll go into the battle, but then we're going home. We're not going to rest in the Promised Land.* They did this little dance and stayed separate from the rest of the nation. Moses rebuked, *Shall your brethren go to war while you sit here? Now why will you discourage the heart of the children of Israel from going over into the land which the LORD has given them?* (verses 6–7) He was afraid that the attitudes of these men were going to discourage the other tribes from going into battle to claim the Promised Land.

These tribes didn't make a very wise choice in the long run. They thought they were doing what was best for their families and that they could have it both ways by living on the outskirts of the Promised Land instead of remaining in the battle with God's people. They made their choice on the basis of fear, personal gain, and comfort. Like Lot (the nephew of Abraham), they walked by sight and not by faith. Matthew 16:25 tells us, *Whoever desires to save his life will lose it, but whoever loses his life for My sake will find it.* Ironically, in trying to keep their families safe and out of the battle, some of them lost the very thing they were trying to save because when enemies attacked Israel, those on the outskirts were the first to get hit. They were prime targets because they were always compromising.

If they had stepped out in faith, crossed over the Jordan, and trusted God's promise of victory, they would have been under God's protection because they would have been in His will. But they were afraid to fight. Sadly, we see that many years later when this battle came about, some of them still hadn't changed. They had unsettled consciences and regrets. They had only visited the Promised Land, but never lived there with their families. Centuries later when Jesus cast demons out of a man and sent them into a herd of pigs, those pigs belonged to descendents of some of these same tribes. The Jews were not to eat pork, but they were raising and eating pigs. Their position on the outskirts of the Promised Land eventually led to their decline.

God wants so much more for us. He wants us to trust Him and to press on. He wants us to enter the Promised Land, claim the victory, and enjoy the blessing. God was faithful to Deborah and Barak, and He used them mightily because they were willing to take that step. Were they afraid? Yes! But they didn't let fear stop them. I wonder if perhaps God is asking you to step out in some area. Is He calling you to take a risk and cross over? God knows and understands your fear. But if you're willing to go, He promises to go with you.

After reading this story I hope you don't conclude, *What a nice story. Isn't God faithful? Look at how faithful He was to Deborah and Barak. How nice.* God wants to take you into the Promised Land. He wants you to walk in victory. He doesn't want you to have regrets and an uneasy conscience twenty years down the road because you were unwilling to grab hold of your kids and go into battle together. They won't learn to fight giants unless you're willing to fight giants. They'll be gripped with fear as long as you are gripped with fear. That's something God spoke to me many, many years ago, and I'm so thankful that He gave me the faith to do what He called me to do. As we learn to walk in victory, we become an example to our children.

Apply the Word to your life. That's when you will see God work, and that's how your faith will grow. Faith comes by hearing the Word, and then by stepping out and obeying it.

Reflections

1. Pause and consider Deborah's courage and faith as she faced a great enemy.
2. In what ways have your faith and courage been tested?
3. How did you respond to the giants you faced and what can you learn from Deborah's example?
4. What does this message communicate about the character of God and in what ways do these attributes inspire you to trust Him more fully?
5. Take a moment to ask the Lord to help you implement these truths in your life today.

About the Author

Cheryl Cahill has been married for twenty-five years to Randy Cahill, senior pastor of Calvary Chapel Boston, Massachusetts.

Calvary Chapel Boston began in their home as a Bible study with eight people and has grown to become the largest church in their area. Randy and Cheryl were born and raised just south of Boston, where they still reside. Cheryl's main ministry is to be a support to her husband and mother to their three grown children. She also oversees Calvary Chapel Boston's women's ministry. Her life verse is Philippians 1:6 . . . *Being confident of this very thing, that He who has begun a good work in you will complete it until the day of Jesus Christ.*

If I could encourage you in anything, it would be to make time for Jesus. That's what we do when someone or something is our priority—we make time for them.

—Diane Coy

Mary and Martha

A Woman of Worship and a Woman of Work

by Diane Coy

---

*As Jesus and his disciples were on their way, he came to a village
where a woman named Martha opened her home to him. She had
a sister called Mary, who sat at the Lord's feet listening to what
he said. But Martha was distracted by all the preparations that
had to be made. She came to him and asked, "Lord, don't you
care that my sister has left me to do the work by myself?
Tell her to help me!"
"Martha, Martha," the Lord answered, "you are worried and
upset about many things, but only one thing is needed. Mary has
chosen what is better, and it will not be taken away from her."*
—Luke 10:38–42, NIV

A friend of mine in Southern California is a pastor's wife
in a growing church and the mother of four preschoolers. The last
thing she needed was the mis-mannered Malamute Husky that she
received as a gift. Fluffy had more energy than her four children
combined and was running wild in her house, chewing everything in
sight. The problem was that her husband and children loved Fluffy.
One day she convinced her husband that it was time to have a family meeting to discuss the puppy's future. Everyone gathered on the
patio and my friend outlined the reasons why this Husky might not
be the best idea for their household. Just then Fluffy ran out of the

playhouse with a sticker from one of the kid's toys on his nose. It said, *God is on my side!* Needless to say, Fluffy stayed!

Today, as in Jesus' day, this is one of the most comforting truths we have: *God is on our side.* This is evident in Jesus' ministry to women. He revolutionized the way women were treated in His culture. At that time, rabbis wouldn't even talk to a woman in public; sometimes they wouldn't even speak to their own wives. But Jesus had female friends, like Mary and Martha of Bethany.

Mary was a woman with an enviable devotional life. She exhibited a lifestyle of devotion rather than a step-by-step formula for growing in Christ. She lived in a very different time and culture, but the Jesus she encountered is the same Jesus who is on our side and ready to meet us today. We have a lot to learn from her! As we consider Mary's life, I want to focus on three main characteristics that we can emulate as women. First, she was a woman of priorities; second, she was a woman with a relationship with Jesus; and third, she was a woman of worship.

In Luke 10:38–42, we see that Mary was a woman of priorities. When I envision this scene, I think about going through my day and suddenly opening the door to Jesus and His disciples after they had been walking in a hot and dusty climate. It seems that I never open the door to unexpected guests when my house is spotless. They always seem to drop by when it's a mess. Mary and Martha opened the door to Jesus and the disciples, who were on their way to Jerusalem. There was a lot of contention surrounding the miracles Jesus performed, so these men were probably exhausted. They needed refreshment, encouragement, and friendship. It was both a great honor and responsibility for these sisters to entertain such a crowd. If I had been in their situation, I would have wanted to create a welcoming atmosphere, but at the same time, so many practical details would have been running through my mind—the water to be drawn, the feet to be washed, the food to be prepared. *Jesus is coming to dinner!*

What would we do if Jesus came to dinner unannounced? This is the scenario Mary and Martha were faced with.

There is an obvious contrast between the attitudes of these two women. When Jesus was sharing with His disciples into the afternoon, Martha was busy serving, but where was Mary? That's what Martha wanted to know! Verse 39 tells us that Mary was at Jesus' feet. In the culture of that day, sitting at someone's feet meant you were accepting that person as a teacher and you were taking the position of pupil or disciple. Mary was listening to Jesus. In the *King James Version*, it says she *heard his word*. The word *heard* means "to give audience and to understand." She wasn't vaguely listening to Him and glancing at Him while at the same time thinking about other things. She was giving audience to what He was saying, hearing His words, and understanding them. In other words, she wasn't being lazy, but was attentive to the Lord. Note the contrast in verse 40— Martha was distracted by all the preparations. That's where I would be. Diane would be distracted by the preparations! I would be thinking about the pitas to be baked and the matzo balls to be made.

I love the Wuest translation of verse 40, which says, *Martha was going around in circles, overly occupied with preparing the meal. And bursting upon Jesus she assumed a stance over Him and said* [her complaint].[1] Can you imagine that? Jesus was ministering to Mary and the disciples while Martha was growing more and more irritated. She was thinking about all she had to do and I'm sure she was giving Mary those looks that sisters give each other that say, *Mary, catch this look over here!* Mary just sat there. In time, resentment began to build up in Martha. If it were me, I would be moving faster and faster, slamming the glasses harder and harder. Then I'd be looking at my sister thinking, *Come on, get with it.* Martha was preoccupied and running in circles,

---

[1] Wuest, Kenneth S. *The New Testament: An Expanded Translation*. Grand Rapids: William B. Eerdmans, 1961.

and then she burst in on Jesus, assumed a stance over Him, and accused Him.

Isn't it interesting that she didn't address Mary but went straight to the Lord with her complaint? When we feel that we're running in circles, we have truly lost sight of the fact that Jesus is in our midst. That's when we begin to grumble and complain. Have you ever gone right to the Lord and accused Him and complained to Him? I've done this many times. My job in the home is to be a professional worrier. Many times I've gone to the Lord and complained, *You gave me a husband with no compassion and no concern for my needs. I need someone who will be concerned and compassionate.* What He has actually done is given me a husband who won't worry with me. One evening Bob came home and shared some heavy-duty things with me that had gone on during his day. That night he went right off to sleep while I stayed awake worrying about these issues. He looked so peaceful. Thinking it wasn't fair, I complained, *Lord, how dare he sleep! He should be up praying with me!* Bob has such trust in the Lord. He knew that God would work everything out for good.

In a similar fashion, Martha burst in on Jesus and began her complaint. She had totally lost sight of the fact that Jesus was in her midst, but Mary hadn't lost sight of the Lord. She wasn't distracted. This is a marvel to me because I have a Martha personality. At first glance, it appears that Mary chose the easier path. The first time I read this Scripture, I thought Jesus was being mean and unfair to Martha. I couldn't understand why she was being rebuked. After all, she was the one doing all the work! Mary was just sitting there when she should have been helping. And yet, Mary chose what was most difficult by taking time to sit at Jesus' feet. She probably knew that Martha was giving her the evil eye. She was probably thinking, *If I don't get up, I'll hear about this. Maybe I should get up. Maybe she's right.* Perhaps she looked about the room and thought of all the things that needed to be done, yet she chose not to be distracted.

A friend once told me that she struggled every morning when she tried to have a devotional time with the Lord. She would sit down, open her Bible, look up and think, *Oh my, that pile of laundry needs to be done,* and would get up, load the washing machine, and then sit down again. Then she'd want a cup of coffee or a glass of water and see the dirty dishes in the sink and would do those before she sat down again. Before she knew it, her devotional time was gone. Finally, she faced her chair towards the corner of the room to avoid these distractions. It worked. Now she doesn't see all the things that need to be done. There have been times when I have been so easily distracted that I have thought that I should put a blanket over my head when I pray.

There are real distractions and responsibilities in our lives. There are children, husbands, pets, housework, church, and service to the Lord, all of which keep us busy—many times too busy. Martha was serving Jesus and that's not a bad thing. He wasn't rebuking her for her service, concern, or ministry style. He was rebuking her for her distraction, her running in circles, and her being overly concerned. Martha was out of balance in her service.

It's so easy to lose our balance. I know this is happening to me when I go to church, look around, and say, *Why didn't somebody do this? Why didn't somebody do that? Doesn't anybody know that I need help over here?* Finally the Lord will whisper, *What are you doing?* I respond, *Serving You.* He gently rebukes, *With that attitude?* God is more interested in our heart attitudes than what we can do for Him in the way of service. We see this in verses 41–42 when He says, *Martha, Martha. You are worried and upset about many things, but only one thing is needed* (NIV). The word *needed* here means "required" or "demanded." One thing is necessary: fellowship with Jesus.

We so often complicate our Christian walk by thinking, *I'm here to love people, to share my faith, to raise children in the Lord, and to serve at my church.* Those things are all good. However, effective service comes through knowing our Lord. First and foremost, the reason we exist is to fellowship with the Lord. Revelation 4:11 tells us that we were created for His good pleasure. Each of us was knit together in our mother's womb for this purpose. God is longing to spend time with us. He has so much He wants to share with us individually. He has so much love to pour upon each of us, and He wants to give us peace. He wants to do so much in our lives, but sometimes we don't even stop to receive.

Mary made the best choice. Every day we make choices. From the time we wake up in the morning until we go to bed each night, we are faced with a multitude of choices. Almost anything that we purchase requires choices: color, shape, size, style, model, price, etc. Sometimes I think life would be so much easier if there were only three colors of dresses and only five different styles, or two car colors and only three styles. Think about how many television channels there are to choose from. Sometimes we choose with wisdom and experience, and sometimes we don't.

I have a lot of fun going to thrift shops, garage sales, and clearance sales, and I love a bargain. When the tag says, *Take an additional 75 percent off,* that's my kind of price! One day Bob and I went to a going-out-of-business sale. They were practically giving things away in order to empty the store. We bought some TV trays that had been floor models for an extra 75 percent off. I was so proud that I had gotten what I thought was the bargain of the century. I went home and set up the trays, only to realize that they weren't the best quality. To this day, I'm afraid to set a meal on them. What appeared to be a bargain was really a waste of money. I made a foolish choice.

Mary chose the best in spite of the cultural wall that she faced. In that day, a woman was not welcome in an educational setting. She sat at the feet of Jesus even though others probably thought she belonged in the kitchen. Maybe she was getting dirty looks, not only from her sister, but also from the men in the room. Women faced domestic barriers, yet the most important thing to Mary was Jesus.

There will always be choices to make between the Lord and the world, the flesh, and the Enemy. When I became a Christian, I never thought that I would have to choose to think about the Lord. He had set me free from so much bondage and turmoil. I had been on the brink of suicide, so I thought I would never forget that I had no life without Him. Yet, as we go on in our Christian walk, somehow we deceive ourselves into thinking that we have arrived because we are good Christian people now. We need to keep making the best choice, and that is spending time with the Lord.

If I could encourage you in anything, it would be to make time for Jesus. That's what we do when someone or something is our priority—we make time for them. There will always be something else to do, so we can't wait for the "right" time. Years ago when Bob was preaching a sermon, it convicted me right to the core. He said, *We all claim to have a personal relationship with Jesus. My question to you today is, "When did your relationship get personal?"* I have never forgotten that question. As I go through my day, week, or month, I constantly ask, *Lord, have I taken time to invest in the personal aspect of our relationship?*

In verse 42, Jesus said, *Mary has chosen what is better, and it will not be taken away from her* (NIV). Like many wise choices, this one comes with a guarantee. Mary invested in the eternal relationship that she had with the Lord. She made an investment that has a return. The dinner, no matter how delicious, was not everlasting. The time Mary spent at Jesus' feet prepared her for the next event, recorded in John chapter 11—the death of her brother Lazarus.

Sitting at the feet of Jesus is not only for times of tragedy, but also for gaining strength to carry our daily burdens. We are not meant to carry them on our own. We can't bear our husbands' burdens, our job responsibilities, or even walk as a Christian on our own. When Jesus talked about taking His yoke in Matthew 11, He was speaking of dependence. The picture is of a two-sided yoke that would be placed on two oxen. One of the oxen would be an older, more mature ox that had already been trained and knew its duty. The other would be a young ox that needed training. The older ox would bear the weight of the burden while the younger ox would simply amble along, learning from the older one. The picture is one of learning to walk a straight path while someone else bears all the weight. We are to let Him bear our burdens! All we need to do is stroll alongside. He has given us the invitation to cast our cares upon Him because He cares for us (1 Peter 5:7). We weren't meant to live this life on our own. We need Him!

John chapter 11 ends so gloriously. Lazarus, Mary and Martha's brother, was raised from the dead. In verse 4, we learn that this situation happened for the glory of God. Verse 45 tells us that many believed on Jesus because of Lazarus' resurrection. Can you even begin to conceive of the celebration and rejoicing that must have unfolded? In that culture, the louder the mourners wailed, the more love it indicated toward the deceased. In fact, people would actually hire mourners to make a lot of noise at their loved one's funeral. Can you picture these professional mourners stunned into silence when Lazarus suddenly walked out of the tomb, and then the awe that must have resounded through the crowd? What an incredible miracle to behold!

We get a glimpse into this celebration in John chapter 12, verses 1–11: *Six days before the Passover, Jesus arrived at Bethany, where Lazarus lived. . . . a dinner was given in Jesus' honor. Martha served, while Lazarus was among those reclining at the table with him. Then Mary took about a pint of pure nard, an expensive perfume; she poured it on Jesus' feet and wiped his feet with her hair. And the house was filled with the fragrance of the perfume. But one of his disciples, Judas Iscariot, who was later to betray him, objected, "Why wasn't this perfume sold and the money given to the poor?" . . . He did not say this because he cared about the poor but because he was a thief; as keeper of the money bag, he used to help himself to what was put into it. "Leave her alone," Jesus replied. "It was intended that she should save this perfume for the day of my burial. You will always* have the poor among you, but you will not always have me." Meanwhile, a large crowd of Jews found out that Jesus was there and came, not only because of him but also to see Lazarus, whom he had raised from the dead. So the chief priests made plans to kill Lazarus as well, for on account of him many of the Jews were going over to Jesus and putting their faith in him (NIV).

Imagine attending this feast and seeing Lazarus. Your attention would be drawn to him as he ate, talked, and sang. You would marvel that he was breathing and living after four days in the tomb. I'm sure that after watching Lazarus, your eyes would focus on the Lord and you would think: *He did this; He truly is God!* Perhaps you would look at Mary or Martha and find them gazing at their brother as well. Imagine the expressions on their faces. Imagine Martha's renewed energy. There would be no complaint from her lips as she was serving this time. What a party and what an incredible sight to behold! Today, when we see someone respond to an altar call, we have the same experience. They were spiritually dead and now they are alive, and we rejoice with the Lord!

Note in verse 1 that this celebration took place six days before Jesus went to the cross. In verse 2, we see that Martha was again serving, but her gift was now in balance. Remember, it's never wrong to be serving the Lord as long as your service is in balance. Where was Mary this time? She was at the feet of Jesus worshiping unreservedly. Once again, she was the lone female in a male-only setting, but she was showing her gratitude. As a Christian, it's so hard to be able to say thank you to the Lord. Words seem so small and empty. I think we can learn something from Mary. She didn't just say thank you. Overwhelmed with gratitude, she gave Jesus her alabaster jar of treasure (some commentators say this expensive perfume represented her dowry). She was so excited that she took action—like when you find the perfect gift for someone and you can't wait to give it to them.

My husband can never wait. A few days before Christmas, he always says, *Do you want your gift now? Do you want to know what it looks like and how big it is?* He gets so excited that he can hardly stand it. I picture Mary, as everyone is talking during the meal, suddenly thinking about the alabaster jar and the beautiful perfume it holds—how she had never used it before, and how perhaps she had been saving it for her wedding. We don't know what plans she had set aside, but after Lazarus was raised from the dead, she decided that her treasure would be used to display her gratitude. Mary came into this celebration and sat at the feet of Jesus. As she admired Him, she broke open the jar to let out the perfume. In that day, alabaster jars weren't opened by taking off the top or loosening the seal. You would actually have to break the jar to pour out the liquid.

Mary's worship was pleasing, simple, and humble. She wasn't concerned about what people thought of her. Otherwise, she probably wouldn't have gone that far in expressing her gratitude. Her worship was costly and risky—Martha was serving, and they had been through this before. The thought must have crossed her mind, *I wonder if Martha will get mad at me again.* Her worship was grateful; it was a thank-you in action. Her worship was Spirit-led. She was undistracted. Imagine this beautiful fragrance filling the room. It probably became quiet, with everyone's attention drawn to Mary and Jesus. Mary's worship was true worship. Worship is much more than singing a song. It is an attitude—a lifestyle. When we worship the Lord in Spirit and truth, our worship will penetrate our office, our home, and our church—whatever setting we're in. As we bring the presence of the Lord with us, His fragrance will fill the room. Many suggest that the alabaster jar that Mary broke open was a symbol of her heart. The kind of worship that pleases the Lord is a broken and open heart before Him.

In verses 4–6, we see a contrast again—this time with Judas Iscariot instead of Martha. Judas objected to Mary's offering because he thought it was a waste of money. He claimed they could have sold the perfume and used the proceeds to minister to the poor. Note that Judas' logic sounded right, but he valued the things of earth while Mary valued her Lord.

Verse 7 says that Jesus came to Mary's defense again. Don't you love that? He had already defended her against Martha and perhaps those who were saying, *Hey, your Jesus failed you in the death of your brother.* As we worship unreservedly, we may be criticized because it's not the way of the world. We can know without a doubt that the Lord will be our defense if our friends or family criticize us. I love when He said that what was done was *intended to happen.* Mary's treasure was intended for His burial even though He was not dead yet. This fragrance was unique in that it could be placed on the skin and the scent would last anywhere from one to two years. How would you like to find perfume like that at the local mall?

When Jesus was arrested, brought to trial, smitten, and had a crown of thorns placed upon His head, the fragrance of that perfume upon His body would have permeated the air. I think that would have given Him such comfort. This act of love performed for His burial stayed with Him. When He was misunderstood and misrepresented, the scent was still upon Him. How magnificent that Mary had the opportunity to be involved in that. Did she truly grasp that Jesus was going to the cross? The disciples never quite comprehended it. I'm not sure that she did either, but I do know that she was Spirit-led because all true acts of worship are born of God's Spirit.

Mark the Lord's words well when He said that she would be remembered for this act of devotion. Women of worship will be remembered. Mark 14:6–9 sheds a different light on this same story. Jesus rebuked Judas and affirmed Mary, saying, *Why are you bothering her? She has done a beautiful thing to me. The poor you will always have with you, and you can help them any time you want. But you will not always have me. She did what she could. She poured perfume on my body beforehand to prepare for my burial. I tell you the truth, wherever the gospel is preached throughout the world, what she has done will also be told, in memory of her* (NIV).

Wherever the gospel is preached, her story will be told. Nearly two thousand years later, we are still giving attention to Mary's act of worship.

I highlighted verse 8 in my Bible where Jesus said, *She did what she could.* I take such encouragement from these words because it is so important to make the choice to spend time with the Lord. You may be thinking, *But you don't know how many distractions I encounter. You don't know how many times I have tried to spend time with the Lord, and it just hasn't happened.* The Lord knows our schedules, He knows our responsibilities, He knows who we share our homes with, He knows our hearts, and we can be sure that He acknowledges those things because He said, *She did what she could.*

My encouragement to you today is to make the choice to do what you can. Whether it's listening to Him, turning to Him in the trials of life, or through an act of worship, make the choice to spend time at His feet.

We are never told anything about Mary's physical appearance. We don't know whether or not she was beautiful. But we do get a glimpse into her heart, and we know that Jesus said she would be remembered for what she did.

The lyrics to one of Charles Wesley's old hymns say, *Oh that I should forever sit with Mary at the Master's feet. Be this my happy choice, my only care, delight and bliss. My joy, my heaven on earth, be this to hear the Bridegroom's voice.* May that be our prayer each day.

Reflections

1. Take a few moments to ponder Mary's devotional lifestyle.
2. Rather than being distracted as Martha was, how can you keep your priorities in order as Mary did?

3. Why is it important for you to prioritize your relationship with Jesus by choosing to sit at His feet?
4. In what ways are you worshipping and what effect is it having on your life?
5. Take a moment to write a prayer or song of worship expressing your gratitude and praise to the Lord.

About the Author

Diane Coy is the wife of Senior Pastor Bob Coy of Calvary Chapel Ft. Lauderdale, Florida. She is also the mother of Christian and Caitlyn, who were both answers to her and Bob's ten-year long prayer for children. Diane is Calvary Chapel born and raised, having accepted Christ under the ministry of Raul Ries when she was eighteen years old. She and Bob left Calvary Chapel Las Vegas, Nevada, in 1985 with one other couple to start the ministry in Ft. Lauderdale. They have had the unique experience of watching God grow their fellowship from four in a living room to thousands on a seventy-eight-acre campus with over four-hundred-thousand square feet of facilities. Diane has overseen the women's ministry at Calvary Chapel Ft. Lauderdale for the last nineteen years, and has taught many Bible studies and conferences. Her style and flavor are reflective of the grace and wisdom with which God has blessed her as she has walked with Him through twenty years of ministry.

—∞—

God created the male/female
relationship because man needs a helper.
For those who are married, this is our
primary responsibility after
glorifying God.

—Cathy Dickinson

—∞—

Job's Wife

A Woman of Grief

by Cathy Dickinson

*Then his wife said to him, "Do you still hold fast to your
integrity? Curse God and die!"
But he said to her, "You speak as one of the foolish women
speaks. Shall we indeed accept good from God, and shall we not
accept adversity?" In all this Job did not sin with his lips.*
—Job 2:9–10

I came across a comparison of men's and women's desires
for their marriage relationship in a book called *His Needs, Her
Needs*. In order of most importance to least, men said they want:
1, sexual fulfillment; 2, recreational companionship; 3, an
attractive spouse; 4, domestic support; and 5, the admiration of
their wives. In contrast, women desire: 1, affection; 2, conversation; 3, honesty and openness; 4, financial support; and 5,
family commitment.[1] Obviously, our goals are very different in
life. Now, if our goals are different, then we are going to behave
differently, aren't we?

When tragedy strikes, people's differences often come into
sharper focus. Job and his wife certainly reacted very differently

[1] Harley, Willard F. Jr. *His Needs, Her Needs: Building an Affair-Proof Marriage*. Grand Rapids:
Fleming H. Revel, 2001.

to the tragedy that befell them. We don't know very much about Job's wife. All we know is that she made this little one-line statement in the Bible to advise her husband when he was down, and because of that statement, we've made what may be unfair conclusions about her character. If we are honest with ourselves, we've all probably, at one time or another, reacted to a difficult situation like this woman did.

Job 1:1 says, *There was a man in the land of Uz, whose name was Job; and that man was blameless and upright, and one who feared God and shunned evil.* Verses 2–5 tell us that Job had ten children and a lot of possessions; God had blessed him abundantly.

Verses 6–12 tell us that Job's circumstances changed drastically: *Now there was a day when the sons of God came to present themselves before the LORD, and Satan also came among them. And the LORD said to Satan, "From where do you come?" So Satan answered the LORD and said, "From going to and fro on the earth, and from walking back and forth on it." Then the LORD said to Satan, "Have you considered My servant Job, that there is none like him on the earth, a blameless and upright man, one who fears God and shuns evil?" So Satan answered the LORD and said, "Does Job fear God for nothing? Have You not made a hedge around him, around his household, and around all that he has on every side? You have blessed the work of his hands, and his possessions have increased in the land. But now, stretch out Your hand and touch all that he has, and he will surely curse You to Your face!" And the LORD said to Satan, "Behold, all that he has is in your power; only do not lay a hand on his person." So Satan went out from the presence of the LORD.*

God gave Satan permission to test Job. He gave him the right to take all that Job had, including his family. But God drew a line that said, *You can take the family, you can take possessions, but you can't touch Job himself.* Verses 13–19 tell us that in one day, Satan took all that he could: *Now there was a day when his sons and daughters were eating and drinking wine in their oldest brother's house; and a messenger came to Job and said, "The oxen were plowing and the donkeys feeding beside them, when the Sabeans raided them and took them away — indeed they have killed the servants with the edge of the sword; and I alone have escaped to tell you!" While he was still speaking, another also came and said, "The fire of God fell from heaven and burned up the sheep and the servants, and consumed them; and I alone have escaped to tell you!" While he was still speaking, another also came and said, "The Chaldeans formed three bands, raided the camels and took them away, yes, and killed the servants with the edge of the sword; and I alone have escaped to tell you!" While he was still speaking, another also came and said, "Your sons and daughters were eating and drinking wine in their oldest brother's house, and suddenly a great wind came from across the wilderness and struck the four corners of the house, and it fell on the young people, and they are dead; and I alone have escaped to tell you!"*

Have you ever had a day like that? You're going along, minding your own business and all of a sudden you get whacked. You pick yourself up, and get knocked right back down. You get up again, and before you're even steady on your feet, you get whacked again. You're thinking, *Wow, what's going on here?* Maybe you have never experienced anything as devastating as Job, but many of us have had days that felt like *whack, whack, whack,* circumstance after circumstance. I've had three days like that in my life. As I look back on them, I realize that they were much like Job's days in that they were real faith testers. During those days, I hung on to a quote from a devotional book that is very precious to me. It said, *Do not let it be said of you that you did not trust God in this.*

According to verses 20–22, Job's trust in God did not fail in the midst of devastating circumstances: *Then Job arose, tore his robe, and shaved his head; and he fell to the ground and worshiped. And he said: "Naked I came from my mother's womb, and naked shall I return there. The LORD gave, and the* LORD *has taken away; Blessed be the name of the* LORD.*" In all this Job did not sin nor charge God with wrong.*

When you're getting whacked right and left, will people be able to say of you, *She trusted God in those circumstances?*

Chapter 2, verses 4–5 tell us that because Satan failed to destroy Job's faith, he went back to the Lord with another proposal: *So Satan answered the* LORD *and said, "Skin for skin! Yes, all that a man has he will give for his life. But stretch out Your hand now, and touch his bone and his flesh, and he will surely curse You to Your face!"* Here is a revelation of a great truth: most men cannot handle sickness. Satan knew that if you want to get to a man, the way to do it is to make him sick. In verses 6–7, God gave him permission to make Job sick: *And the* LORD *said to Satan, "Behold, he is in your hand, but spare his life." So Satan went out from the presence of the* LORD, *and struck Job with painful boils from the sole of his foot to the crown of his head.*

Notice that Satan took everything from Job: his possessions, his health, and every family member, except one. Satan did not take Job's wife even though he had permission. Now, why do you think Satan made that decision? I believe his goal was to get Job to break—to get him to a place of such misery that he would curse God to His face (1:11, 2:5).

Satan's goals and tactics have not changed much over the years. He's still trying to get us to curse God, using the strategy we read about in Job. He brings rough trials into our lives, and then he brings somebody to plead his cause. Most of us don't even realize when we are being used as a tool of the Enemy. This is where Mrs. Job comes into the picture: *Then his wife said to him, "Do you still hold fast to your integrity? Curse God and die!"* (2:9) Satan's goal was to get Job to curse God, and his beloved wife, who was supposed to be his greatest supporter, was instead a weapon of the Enemy. She tried to convince Job to do the very thing that Satan wanted him to do. She said, *Curse God, Job. Get this over with.* There it is—one little sentence. When push came to shove, Job's wife yielded to the voice of the Enemy and became his instrument.

My question to you is this: whose instrument are you in the lives of others? God created the male/female relationship because man needs a helper. For those who are married, this is our primary responsibility after glorifying God. He created us to support and help our husbands (Genesis 2:18). They desire us to be their cheerleaders. I once heard a tape of Andy Stanley, son of the Southern Baptist preacher Charles Stanley, in which he said, *In some ways we guys never grow up. When I was in high school, my desire was to be on the football field and to hear my girlfriend yell, "Yea! Go Andy, Go! You're the best!"* He concluded, *Men never lose the desire to have a woman behind them saying "Go! You're the best!"*

Our job is to cheer our husbands on and support them. I've looked and I can't find anywhere in Scripture where it says, *Women, correct your husbands. Women, change your husbands. Women, it's your job to see that they do things right.* And yet, we often think we are the best instrument to promote change in their lives because we live with them. It makes so much sense to us, but God says, *Back off. It's My job to change him. Your job, wife, is to be his supporter and cheerleader.*

The world is beating our husbands up, and they need us to build them up and tell them they are wonderful. I'm not saying we can't offer advice or even correction once in a while. My question is: What are you known for? Would your husband describe you as the person who generally brings him down or the one who is out to fix him? Would he say, *You know, when everybody else is against me, I know you'll be there? I know that when I make a mistake, you may not agree with me, but you'll support me and hang in there with me.*

Women have had a great influence over men throughout the ages, and not always for good. In Genesis 3:17, God said to

Adam, *Because you have heeded the voice of your wife, and have eaten from the tree of which I commanded you, saying, "You shall not eat of it": cursed is the ground for your sake; in toil you shall eat of it all the days of your life.* Adam fell because he listened to Eve. And, remember Sarah's brilliant idea that Abraham should fulfill the promise of God by having a son with Hagar? We come up with what we think are such brilliant ideas, and we have great power over the men in our lives to implement them.

Although marriage is the primary place where married women are called to be supporters, we are all called to be supportive of others in every walk of life. Job's wife said, *Why don't you just curse God and die?* She failed to influence her husband in this situation, but her words ought to challenge us to ask ourselves how we are doing in this area. Job's reply appears in verse 10: *He said to her, "You speak as one of the foolish women speaks. Shall we indeed accept good from God, and shall we not accept adversity?" In all this, Job did not sin with his lips.*

We sometimes forget that these horrible things didn't just happen to Job. His wife had lost everything too; she had lost ten children and her home. The only difference was that she kept her health. But she had experienced a great tragedy and her husband didn't seem to be doing anything about it. He was accepting what had happened to them. He refused to challenge God for what He had allowed them to suffer. She probably felt like he was handling it all wrong. I don't know what Mrs. Job did right after this; nobody does. The Bible doesn't mention her ever again. But right after Mr. and Mrs. Job had this little conversation, Job's three friends entered the picture because they had heard of all the adversity that had come upon Job (2:11). We don't know how they heard the news. This was a big tragedy that befell an affluent man, so the news probably spread fast. I wonder if they heard all these things from Mrs. Job. Did she go to them and say, *Hey, talk to Job. See if you can find out why this happened—what he's doing wrong. Get him to take care of me. Get him to do something!* I'm only speculating, but as women, we can be so manipulative.

Notice that throughout this trial, Job chose the companionship of his three friends over that of his wife. Are you a safe place for your husband when he is hurting? Is your home a refuge for him? Is it a place where he would rather be than anywhere else? It should be. Many men choose to run to other things rather than to the home as a refuge, and we as wives can have a lot to do with their choice. It's a good check for us every once in a while to think about our home life and to ask ourselves: *What am I like? Am I a safe place for him? Am I the person he wants to be with when he's hurting, or am I someone that he wants to get away from when things are going badly?* Are his thoughts safe with you? Is having a conversation with you something he can look forward to, or does he regret that he shared his heart with you? Is he treated like the king of the house, or does he walk in feeling like the bad guy?

If Job had given in to his wife's suggestion to curse God, what do you think would have happened? She said, *Curse God and die.* Obviously, she believed death would come next. Fortunately, we live in the age of grace in which God is very merciful and longsuffering toward us. For some reason, He allows us to curse Him and doubt Him. I once listened to a testimony tape in which Kay Arthur said that one night before she came to the Lord she shook her fist at God and said, *To hell with You, God.* I heard that and thought, *Whoa.* She said that in her spirit she felt like God replied, *To heaven with you, Kay.* And He saved her soul. He is so gracious and patient, but there are also consequences for doubting and cursing God.

Perhaps one consequence is that we lose the attitude of being thankful. Romans 1:20–26 says, *From the time the world was created, people have seen the earth and sky and all that God made. They can clearly see his invisible qualities—his eternal power and divine nature. So they have no excuse whatsoever for not knowing God. Yes, they knew God, but they wouldn't worship him as God or even give him thanks. And they began to think up foolish ideas of what God was like. The result was that their minds became dark and confused. Claiming to be wise, they became utter fools instead. And instead of worshiping the glorious, ever-living God, they worshiped idols made to look like mere people, or birds and animals and snakes. So God let them go ahead and do whatever shameful things their hearts desired. As a result, they did vile and degrading things with each other's bodies. Instead of believing what they knew was the truth about God, they deliberately chose to believe lies. So they worshiped the things God made but not the Creator himself, who is to be praised forever. Amen. That is why God abandoned them to their shameful desires* (NLT).

This passage is typically applied to unbelievers, but we as believers can fall into this same wickedness. These verses are basically describing a group of people who refuse to thank God, or to worship and accept Him. They came up with their own idea of what He's like. Job's friends did the same thing. They asked Job, *What did you do wrong?* And concluded, *Bad things are happening to you; therefore, God is punishing you.* Was that truth? No, it was their false idea of God. In the beginning of the book of Job, God had declared that Job was righteous and blameless. Even so, bad things were happening to him. We do the same thing when we attribute motives to God that aren't true, when we forget to thank Him, or when we seek fulfillment from other sources. As a result of this kind of mindset, God gave those described in Romans 1 up to their own thinking. He sometimes does the same thing to us as Christians: *Okay, you want to think that way? Go ahead.*

Aren't you afraid of the way you think? I'm afraid of the way I think because I don't think right. I'm selfish. I'm prideful. In my flesh, I want to blame God and doubt Him. If Satan can get us to the place of being left to our own thinking, then he begins to win because we are thinking like him. He can lead us to the place he wanted Job to be—where we blame and curse God, and spiral down into bondage.

Scripture is full of exhortations to bless God and encourage others to do so. Proverbs 12:25 says, *Anxiety in the heart of man causes depression, but a good word makes it glad.* Proverbs 15:23 exhorts, *A man has joy by the answer of his mouth, and a word spoken in due season, how good it is!* Proverbs 25:11 says, *A word fitly spoken is like apples of gold in settings of silver.* Second Corinthians 1:3–4 declares, *Blessed be the God and Father of our Lord Jesus Christ, the Father of mercies and God of all comfort, who comforts us in all our tribulation, that we may be able to comfort those who are in any trouble, with the comfort with which we ourselves are comforted by God.* And 2 Corinthians 13:11 says, *Finally, brethren, farewell. Become complete. Be of good comfort. Be of one mind, live in peace; and the God of love and peace will be with you.*

The word *comfort* in these last two verses means "to encourage one another." It comes from the root of the Greek word *paraclete*, which means "to come alongside." The same word is used to describe the Holy Spirit, who is the best comforter. We are encouraged to come alongside one another as the Holy Spirit does, comforting and encouraging one another, and being kind to one another.

Twila Paris sings a song about friendship that includes these lines: *You are a true friend pointing me to Him, lifting my downcast eyes, turning my wondering gaze to the sky, proving your love again. You are a true friend.*[2] A true friend comes alongside like the Holy Spirit and pulls a person away from looking down or looking around, and gets them looking upward to Jesus again. That's what Job needed, and that's

[2] Paris, Twila. "True Friend," *For Every Heart*, 1988.

what we all need from one another. Satan's goal is to get us to curse God, but God wants us to bless Him.

As I said, we often think like Satan. Our natural tendency is to curse, blame, and question God. It's not natural for us to bless Him, praise Him, and trust Him. That's why the Bible has to tell us to do it. Any time we are told to do something in Scripture, we are being commanded to do something that doesn't come naturally. God has to remind us of the way we're supposed to live. In Psalm 103, David told himself, *Bless the Lord, O my soul.* He instructed himself to do what was not natural for him. When he strengthened himself in the Lord, he was encouraged. One way to do this is to bless God in difficult times rather than curse Him. Job 2:10 says, *In all this Job did not sin with his lips,* but we can't say that about his wife, can we?

What are you choosing to do with your lips? What choices are you making as you come alongside others? Are you a vessel for God's purposes or are you an instrument of the Devil in the lives of others? Are you known by your family, friends, and co-workers as one who encourages or one who discourages? What do they anticipate when they think about having a conversation with you? *She's going to bring me up,* or *She's going to bring me down?* We don't want to be like Job's wife. She was a discouragement and an instrument of the Enemy. We want to be like Job who did not sin with his lips.

Reflections

1. Pause and reflect on the story of Job's wife and her relationship with her husband.

2. Contrast her response to tragedy with that of her husband. What lessons can you learn from this?

3. How are you being used as an instrument of encouragement or discouragement to others?
4. List the steps you can take to develop a right way of thinking.
5. What results can you expect when you bless, praise, and trust God? Stop and write your prayer expressing those thoughts to Him.

About the Author

Cathy Dickinson has been married to Dale Dickinson, senior pastor of Calvary Chapel of El Cajon, California, for thirty-four years. She has two married children and three grandchildren.

Cathy began attending Calvary Chapel Costa Mesa in 1973. Dale was an assistant pastor at Calvary Chapel Costa Mesa before they moved to El Cajon in 1997, and Cathy served there as a women's and marriage counselor, and wrote many of the lessons for the Joyful Life Bible studies. She currently writes the homework and teaches the women's Bible study at Calvary Chapel El Cajon. She continues to counsel women, and, together with Dale, married couples.

There is no greater joy besides knowing the Lord than knowing others who know Him. It is through the eyes of another devoted follower that we see a different facet in the prism of who Jesus is, and our knowledge of Him is enhanced.

—Cathe Laurie

Mary Magdalene

A Woman Transformed

by Cathe Laurie

Then they said to her, "Woman, why are you weeping?"
She said to them, "Because they have taken away my Lord, and I
do not know where they have laid Him."
Jesus said to her, "Mary!"
She turned and said to Him, "Rabboni!" (which is to say,
Teacher).
—John 20:13, 16

When I look at before-and-after photographs of women who get makeovers, I think, *Wow! What a difference.* I react the same way to Mary Magdalene. Her life demonstrates the magnificence of Jesus Christ's resurrection. The many extraordinary qualities in her character challenge me as a Christian woman who wants to follow and love the Lord. She is an incredible example of a before-and-after transformation, but hers was not the result of a new hairstyle, magic at the cosmetic counter with brushes and paint, or a diet program. Mary's heart was transformed by the power of the Holy Spirit.

Similar makeovers happen in lives today. I've met people before they came to Christ who may not have changed their makeup, hair color, or clothing, but after an encounter with Jesus, their lives changed from within, and it altered their outer appearance. The reverse is true as well. I've seen people turn back from walking with the Lord, and it showed on their faces. That is really tragic. In Mary's life, we never read about any lapse of faith. When she gave her heart to the Lord, she gave all of it, following Him to the very end.

There are several women named Mary in the New Testament, but Mary Magdalene is unique. Perhaps God inspired the New Testament writers to leave out the details of her life before she came to Christ because of her devotion and love after her conversion. All we know for certain is that she came from a town called Magdala and that she was possessed by seven demons. Some commentators have said that the number seven is symbolic rather than literal, indicating that her life was completely controlled and taken over by many demons (seven being the number of completion or totality in Scripture). How this demonic possession was manifested, we don't know, but get images of Linda Blair from the movie, *The Exorcist*, out of your mind. New Testament portrayals of demon possession include muteness, deafness, blindness, anger, aggression, fierceness, unusual strength, and convulsions.

One graphic picture of a man possessed with many demons is the man from Gadara (Luke 8). I love this story because I can easily envision this sad, pathetic man. His life was in total shambles. He lived naked in the wilderness among the tombs that were carved out of the mountains. People had tried to bind him with ropes, chains, or wooden stocks, perhaps hoping to control him, but he would break free. He would cut and tear at his own body. Self-mutilation was a symptom of his demon possession. He wandered day and night in the mountains crying out with a loud voice. Can you imagine? He was an outcast of outcasts, and no one was able to help him.

Then he had an encounter with Jesus and was delivered from the legion of demons that possessed him. Immediately afterwards, the man was sitting clothed and in his right mind at Jesus' feet. Later we read that he actually pleaded with Jesus to be allowed to follow Him and become one of His disciples. What an amazing transformation the love and compassion of Jesus affected in this man. Like Mary, he was given a commission to go and tell others about the great things the Lord had done for him. Although we don't know for sure what symptoms of demon possession Mary experienced, we do know they were both tragic and total.

Mary's environment may have contributed to her downfall. The city of Magdala cannot be found today, but historians have determined that it was on the west side of the Sea of Galilee in the northern region of Israel. At the time of Christ, it was a thriving city located on a trade route between two Roman stronghold cities: Tiberias and Capernaum. Magdala is mentioned only once in Scripture, in Matthew 15:39. After the feeding of the four thousand, Jesus got into a boat and went to the area of Magdala.

Because of her name, we can reasonably assume that Mary was of Jewish lineage. It would have been a challenge for Jews to live in Galilee and hold on to their faith because it was a secular region far from the religious life of the Temple in Jerusalem. Imagine trying to raise a daughter to be pure amidst the temptations so common to a secular city.

According to Jewish history, Magdala was a town in which prostitution was quite prevalent. This may have given rise to the church tradition of identifying Mary as an immoral woman, but there is nothing in Scripture that teaches this for certain. Another possible reason for this tradition lies in the fact that Mary Magdalene is first introduced in Luke 8, directly after the story of the immoral woman who ministered to Jesus at the end of chapter 7.

The before-picture of Mary's life is blurry at best. We don't know anything about her family, age, or profession. However, she must have had some means of livelihood that enabled her to support Jesus' ministry and travel extensively with Him and the disciples. In thinking about what might have opened the door to her demonic possession, I am reminded that those of us who are trying to raise our children for the Lord need to be aware of the subtlety of the Enemy's tactics. We're living in an age when anything religious is acceptable: the New Age movement, worship of angels, astrology, the Harry Potter entertainment franchise, even playing with Ouija boards. We really need to have our guard up because these things can make it seem acceptable to toy with the occult.

I have a good friend who hired a "Christian" tutor to help her home-schooled daughter. This tutor took the little girl to breakfast one day and introduced her to a friend. The tutor left the table to get some hot chocolate and when she returned this "friend" had the little girl in tears. She had just lost her older sister in a tragic car accident and was in a very vulnerable place. The tutor's friend had heard about her sister's death. During their conversation, she told the little girl that angels speak to her and actually said, *I have wanted to meet you because I have a message for you from your sister: she wants you to know that she's okay.*

Anyone grieving the loss of a close family member might be tempted to respond, *Yes! You have a message for me! Where are they? How are they? What are they doing? What is it like?* For this little girl, any of those questions would be understandable. She wanted so much to see her sister again. But, she was spiritually sensitive and discerning enough to realize that there was no mention of Jesus in this conversation. It was all about angels.

Needless to say, when my friend found out about this, she put a complete stop to it. The teacher was dismissed with a rebuke: *How dare you expose my daughter to this! You have no idea what she is going through. How can you call yourself a Christian?* The woman said that she believed she had a gift with children, and that the minister in her church was completely aware of her unscriptural views on angels. I wonder how many unsuspecting, naïve Christians and children have tragically fallen into the trap of communicating with angels. If these so-called angels are anything beyond invented stories, they would be demonic forces. An encounter like this could be an open door through which one could easily slip into bondage. We don't know what occurred in Mary's life, but at some point she had an encounter with demonic forces and was completely given over to them.

Mary is introduced into Scripture in Luke 8: *After this, Jesus traveled about from one town and village to another, proclaiming the good news of the kingdom of God. The Twelve were with him, and also some women who had been cured of evil spirits and diseases: Mary (called Magdalene) from whom seven demons had come out; Joanna the wife of Cuza, the manager of Herod's household; and Susanna; and many others* (verses 1–3, NIV).

There are fourteen references made to her in the New Testament. She is mentioned first in eight of those references, which means she was featured prominently among this elite group of women disciples. Mary was so transformed from a life of demonic possession that she stood out. We don't know how, when, or where her encounter with Jesus took place, but the Bible provides us with an incredible *after* shot of this amazing woman who was given a new life and a new heart.

I read the true story of South African heart surgeon Christian Barnard, who performed the world's first heart transplant. He asked one of his transplant patients, *Would you like to see your old heart?* The patient said, *Yes, I would.* So at 8:00 p.m. one evening, they went to a room at the Groote Shuur Hospital in Cape Town, South Africa. Dr. Barnard opened a cupboard, took out a glass container, and handed it to the patient. Inside was his old heart. For a moment, the patient stood there stunned and silent as they examined it. He was the first man to ever hold his own heart in his hand. After several minutes, he said, *So this is my old heart which caused me so much trouble,* then handed it back to the doctor, turned away, and left it forever.[1]

What an incredible picture of what Mary Magdalene did with her old life! She looked at the shambles that had been her heart, then turned and left it forever to begin anew. The heart that Christ gave her loved with such a love. She loved Jesus the way He wanted to be loved. And how is it that Jesus wants to be loved?

First, we see that Mary wanted to be with Him. She became His devoted follower. Luke 8:1 says, *The Twelve were with him and also some women.* When I read that I wondered if the word *with* refers to anything beyond the obvious in this verse. I studied the different Greek words that are translated *with* in our English language. The Greek word *meta* means "amidst." For example, if we are in a room together, we're in the midst of one another. Another Greek word, *para*, means "beside," which sounds as if it might indicate a closer relationship, like two women sitting together in the front row of a church service. But the word for *with* in this passage means "united with." It's more than being in the midst of, or beside someone. It means "a uniting of heart, mind, and purpose." Mary was transformed. She was devoted and now she

---

[1] "Christian Barnard." Posted February 23, 2004. *Nationmaster.com. www.nationmaster.com.* (Accessed August 9, 2004.)

was united to the Lord. How does this uniting of heart, mind, and purpose behave? This is an important question because if you believe in Jesus, it's going to affect your behavior.

We read that *she followed Him* (see Matthew 27:55–56). That was one way that she behaved. Think of what it means to follow someone. Following my husband, Greg, on the freeway in a car or following behind someone on my bicycle can be very challenging. Greg would say he is a more "skilled" driver than I am. Borrowing a description I once heard, I would say he is a more "enthusiastic" driver. I have to pay attention when I'm following him on the freeway because there's always the chance, when I don't know where I am going, that he's going to pull off at the next exit and I'll lose him. I want to be right behind his car and I don't want other people to cut in and block my vision. It's easy to get a couple of cars back, and then get lost. Because Mary wanted to be intimately united with Jesus, she closely followed Him.

I ride bikes with some incredibly skilled riders. I like to follow behind them because I know they're going to be careful and point out anything in the road that might cause me to crash. They are going to use hand signals to tell me when they're slowing down, or when we need to go single file. They're going to be cuing me throughout the ride, *Heads up, Rider right, Car left*, or *Car back*. I want to be close enough to hear their warnings, along with their stories and inside tips. I also want to be in range to benefit from the draft they create because on a bicycle you can save 20 percent of your energy by riding on someone else's wheel. But I don't want to draft behind just anyone. I must have confidence in the person I'm drafting behind because some people are all over the road. They are dangerous cyclists and I won't have anything to do with them.

I bet that if Jesus was nearby, Mary wanted to be right behind Him. She wanted to be close enough to hear everything He had to say. She was a follower. When Jesus slowed down, she slowed down. When He sped up, she sped up. When He instructed her to do something, she did it. He had given her a new life, and it was her joy to love Him the way He wanted to be loved by being *with* Him.

Second, Mary learned what Jesus loved and gained perspective by listening to His words. She wanted to be with Him because she wanted to know Him. The followers of Jesus who were united with Him sometimes heard Him herald and proclaim, or preach. At other times, they heard Him declare or show glad tidings. They heard Him simply talk. In whatever manner Jesus was communicating with His disciples, Mary wanted to understand. As a matter of fact, when Jesus appeared to her at the tomb and she finally recognized Him, she called him *Rabboni*, which means "teacher." He had what she wanted to know, and so she learned what He loved.

She was close enough to listen. Have you ever been in a conversation at a dinner table, seated next to one person, but you really wanted to hear someone else's conversation? There are times when my husband Greg and I are out to dinner with friends and the girls all sit at one side of the table and the guys all sit at the other side. Most of the time I don't mind, but every once in a while the guys are having a much more interesting conversation. I'm half listening to what the girls are saying, and trying to seem interested, but the other half of me is zoning in on the conversation across the table. The older I get, the noisier restaurants get, so it is a real challenge to hear everything.

One time Greg was having a conversation with someone in another room, and I was not invited to be a part of the discussion, but I confess, I was so interested! I pressed my ear right up against the door, but as I was listening, Greg became suspicious. In the middle of his conversation, he got up and opened the door, and I just about fell into the room! Greg looked at me, and said,

Oh, brother! Then he shut the door. I was so embarrassed, but when you want to hear something, you're willing to do just about anything! Mary really wanted to hear and she learned what Jesus loved because she listened to Him.

Third, Mary loved the people Jesus loved. She was close to Jesus, but she was also close to His disciples. Mary was always in the company of women that traveled with Jesus. Some of them are mentioned by name: Salome, Mary the mother of James and Joses, Joanna, and Susanna were among her good friends and partners in ministry. It's such a blessing to read that. There is no greater joy besides knowing the Lord than knowing others who know Him. It is through the eyes of another devoted follower that we see a different facet in the prism of who Jesus is, and our knowledge of Him is enhanced.

The great thing about friendship, when it's based on the Lord, is that it's *the more, the merrier.* Friends who share the same interests, goals, and vision are not jealous when another person joins the group. Real friendship is not exclusive and cliquish. That's turning inward. Friends with the same focus and vision are looking outward, and welcome new people into the circle. In ministry and in close Christian friendships, you begin to appreciate what one friend will bring out in another friend. Have you ever noticed that? C. S. Lewis said, *For a Christian, there are strictly speaking no chances. Jesus said to His disciples, You haven't chosen Me, but I have chosen You. He could easily say of a group of Christian friends, You haven't chosen one another, I have chosen you for one another.*[2] Jesus orchestrates our friendships, and what a joy that is.

Mary loved the people Jesus loved. Are you comfortable around godly people? Who are your close friends? Who do you choose to hang around with? Are you more at home with non-believers and marginal Christians than with those who are truly passionate about

---

[2] Lewis, C. S. *The Four Loves.* New York: Harcourt Brace, 1960.

the Lord? Love those whom He loves and build yourself up spiritually through those relationships.

Fourth, Scripture says, *She ministered to Him* (see Mark 15:41). She loved Him how He wanted to be loved by ministering to Him. The word *ministered* means "to serve, support, wait upon, or attend to as a host or a friend would." It's the same word used to describe the service of deacons in the New Testament. Mary and her friends were servants and helpers. What did their service look like? We can only imagine that as a group of women they did certain things that women generally do better than men. I won't say all women do these things better than men do, but by and large, there are certain things that women can do better. Mary and her friends might have done the shopping, the cooking, the sewing, the washing, the cleaning, and the event planning. They did what they were best equipped to do. For those of us who want to love Jesus in the way He wants to be loved, we must look at our own lives and ask ourselves: *What gifts and talents do I possess? Where are my strengths? Can I use those in the kingdom of God to love Him how He wants to be loved?*

Mary was involved in ministry, and because she loved, she was dependable. When Mary was given a job to do, I have no doubt that she showed up on time and got to work. She didn't stand around talking. She rolled up her sleeves, and stayed until the job was done. I'm sure she was dependable in her service because she was serving Him. What a great privilege. Wouldn't it have been amazing to wash Jesus' robe, sew a tear in His clothing, or cook a meal for Him? It's tempting to say, *Mary had that privilege, but Jesus isn't around in bodily form for me to serve.*

Jesus said, *If you do it to the least of these My brothers, you've done it unto Me* (see Matthew 25:40). That could refer to your husband, your children, or your co-workers. We are to serve the people around us in whatever sphere God has placed us. When service gets tough, the secret to submission is doing it for Him. I always fall back on this verse because I want to be faithful and dependable. If I'm doing it for my kids, for Greg, for the church, or for whomever, I'm doing it for the Lord. Ruth Graham had a sign over her kitchen sink that said, *Divine service done three times a day.* When she was doing those dishes, it was a reminder that if she was doing them as unto the Lord, it was divine service. God will reward you for that attitude. I think it is truly the motivating factor in doing what we do well.

Fifth, how did Jesus want to be loved? He wanted all her possessions to be available to Him. Mary and the other women evidently had means beyond what was necessary to support themselves, and were able to give materially to the ministry of Jesus. He and the disciples fished, but didn't hold regular jobs during their three years of public ministry. The women supported them. We don't know the source of their money—perhaps they sold their property, or had some regular income. The important point is that Mary loved generously, so she gave generously, serving Jesus with her resources.

Early in the nineteenth century, the king of Prussia, Frederick William III, was in trouble. His country was surrounded by nations seeking to gain dominance, and he was fighting wars, but running out of resources to finance them. The king asked Prussian women to give their gold, silver, and jewelry to fund the defense of their country. In exchange for their jewelry and precious metals, the king gave them ornaments made of iron. Inscribed on the ornaments were the words: *I gave gold for iron—1813.*

The response was overwhelming. The women gladly brought their jewelry. Nobody could have expected what happened as a result. Prussian women came to prize that gift from their king more than they did their jewelry, and history records that in the nineteenth century, wearing jewelry became unfashionable for Prussian women. Women with the iron cross formed an elite group called *The Order of the Iron Cross*. To this day, it is traditional among members to refrain from wearing jewelry. The moral of this story is that we need more women today who are so committed to the King of kings that they would willingly give of their resources—not only monetary resources, but whatever they have of value, thus demonstrating their deep devotion to their King.[3]

In a sense, Mary turned her checkbook over to Jesus. At tax time, it can be a sad eye-opener to realize how much money we have spent on restaurant meals, clothing, and other luxuries compared to what we have given to the work of the ministry. I once heard Alan Redpath say, *You watch a man with his checkbook, and you'll know where his priorities lie.* These women gave their resources from a debt of gratitude. What are we willing to turn over to Him?

Sixth, Mary loved courageously. Unlike the disciples who fled in fear, when Jesus was arrested, Mary followed Him to the mock trial before Pilate. She followed Him along the Via Dolorosa. She watched Him stumble under the weight of the cross. She watched Him bleed. She heard Him say, *Daughters of Jerusalem, do not weep for Me* (Luke 23:28). She watched as He was nailed to the cross. She watched them pierce His side. At first Mary and the others stood afar off, but by the time Jesus uttered His first statements from the cross: *Father, forgive them* (Luke 23:34), and *Woman, behold your son* (John 19:26)—Mary was at His feet. She watched Him die, but even then she wouldn't leave Him.

It was Mary's joy in life to tend to Jesus' needs—to wash His clothing, prepare His meals, or do whatever He required.

---

[3] Kulp, George B. "Nuggets of Gold." Posted May 31, 2004. *Rapture Ready. www.rap-tureme.com.* (Accessed August 5, 2004.)

Suddenly He was gone, but still she waited at the foot of the cross. She only had His dead body, but she held on to the responsibility of ministering to Him and caring for His needs. She waited until Joseph of Arimathea received permission to take His body down and bury it. John's gospel mentions the fact that he and Nicodemus brought fresh linen to wrap the body, along with one hundred pounds of myrrh and aloes or spices. Mary watched as they took Jesus' body from the cross, wrapped it, anointed it, and laid it in the tomb. She followed His body until she was prevented by the Sabbath from staying any longer. Finally, she left Him. This had to be Mary's darkest day ever. I don't know how much she comprehended about His death and resurrection, but her confusion must have been overwhelming at that moment.

When the Sabbath was over, Mary went right back to where she had last seen Jesus' body. Very early on Sunday morning, she and the other women brought more spices to anoint His body. As they walked through the darkness, the women were talking amongst themselves: *How are we going to move this huge stone? Who is going to help us?* Their prayers were answered, perhaps even before they had a chance to express them. There had been a great earthquake and the stone was rolled away by an angel. When the women arrived at the tomb and saw that it was empty, Mary immediately thought someone had taken the body of Jesus. She was absolutely beside herself. She ran to Peter and John, and said to them, *They have taken away the Lord out of the tomb, and we do not know where they have laid Him* (John 20:2). Peter and John ran to the tomb. Peter carefully examined the linen wrappings that had been used to bury Jesus. John didn't enter the tomb, but peeked in and saw for himself that Jesus' body was gone. The men left, and went back to their homes, but Mary didn't leave. Mary had nowhere to go. She sat weeping outside the sepulcher.

Mary showed such devotion. She was willing and wanting to love beyond what was required. She loved Jesus lavishly. In her mind, one hundred pounds of aloe wasn't enough to anoint His body and she brought even more. You might wonder, *Now, why would anyone do that?* In Mary's mind, it was her last chance to do something for her Lord, and she wasn't going to let it pass by, so she brought even more than was necessary. She was overcome with grief when she realized that her opportunity was taken from her.

John 20:12 tells us that she saw two angels—one at the head and the other at the foot of where Jesus' body had been lying. They asked her, *Woman, why are you weeping?* She answered, *Because they have taken away my Lord, and I don't know where they have laid Him* (verse 13). After she said this, she turned and saw Jesus standing there, but she didn't recognize Him. He too asked, *Woman, why are weeping? Whom are you seeking?* (verse 15) When a statement or idea is repeated in Scripture, it is often done for emphasis. Jesus challenged Mary to really think about why she was there, and whom she was seeking. Was it just a body? Was it just a man? Was it just a teacher? Was it just someone who affected her life? He wanted her to examine her purpose for being there.

She had loved in a tangible, physical way by working with her hands, but her relationship with Jesus had to change. It had to pass from one phase to another. It had to become a different kind of loving, a different kind of serving. That's what Jesus was calling her attention to. Supposing Him to be the gardener, she said, *Sir, if You have carried Him away, tell me where You have laid Him, and I will take Him away* (verse 15). Hers was the kind of love that was supernatural in its desire to do what it could not physically do. Think about it. There was no way Mary could have carried Jesus' body all by herself, yet she was willing. Then Jesus called her name, *Mary,* and she turned and said, *Rabboni! . . . Teacher* (verse 16). At that point, she was going to love Him until her desire was satisfied.

Psalm 63:1 tells us that those who seek Him early will find Him. Mary was seeking the Lord, and she was going to discover Him in a whole new way. The last time that we read Mary's name in the gospel account, we see her clinging to Jesus. He said to her, *Mary, don't cling to Me.* In some translations it says, *Touch me not.* He then said, *I have not yet ascended to My Father; but go to My brethren and say to them, "I am ascending to My Father and your Father, to My God and your God"* (verse 17). He was pointing her to that spiritual relationship that she would need and helping her understand how she must relate to Him from that time forward. He commissioned her as the first evangelist of the New Testament with a message of the risen Savior. What an awesome privilege! I think that was love's reward, the greatest of all privileges—telling others the good news. The dark night she had passed through hadn't been in vain, and Mary was captured forever in the light of that beautiful Easter morning as she was given one last word from Jesus for His disciples. What an encouraging word it was!

Perhaps today you are wondering what it is that God wants you to do. We can look at the life of Mary and learn so much from her about how Jesus wants to be loved. He wants us to love Him by following Him closely, by listening and learning, by loving those whom He loves, and by loving steadfastly and hanging in there when things get tough. He wants us to love Him by serving and giving generously of what is precious, by persevering to the end, and by loving until we are satisfied. I thank the Lord for Mary's example because it challenges me in a most profound way to go out and take hold of all that He has for me.

Perhaps you love someone that has not yet been transformed like Mary was when she met Jesus. They're in bondage and their life seems to be a shambles. Believe that God is able to make them over completely just as He did Mary. Never give up on them.

What an honor and privilege to have this before-and-after picture to challenge and inspire us. Through it God gives us the charge to go and tell the good news of His gospel. May our lives be the kind of witness that we see in Mary's life. If there are areas that you are holding on to, areas that you have not yet surrendered to Jesus, may you willingly hand them over today. And may you prize ever so dearly what He will give you in exchange: the gift of knowing that He is pleased.

Reflections

1. Take a moment and reflect on the life of Mary Magdalene.
2. How are you inspired by her transformed life?
3. There are six spiritual principles given in this message for loving Jesus: 1, follow Him; 2, listen to Him; 3, love those He loved; 4, serve Him; 5, give generously; 6, love courageously. In which of these areas are you weak and in which are you strong?
4. What changes do you need to make in order to love Him as passionately as Mary did?
5. Make this your prayer to renew your love relationship with Jesus.

About the Author

Cathe Laurie was born in Long Beach, California, and grew up in Southeast Asia. She returned to California in ninth grade, went to Calvary Chapel Costa Mesa when it met in the little chapel on Sunflower Avenue, and was saved in the Jesus Movement. Cathe married her husband, Greg Laurie, pastor of seventeen-thousand member Harvest Christian Fellowship in Riverside, California, when she was eighteen years old. She has been a pastor's wife for thirty-one years and oversees Harvest's women's ministry, which reaches two thousand women. Cathe and Greg have two sons, Christopher (29) and Jonathan (18).

God is not looking for perfect people to perform His wonders and accomplish His eternal purposes. He is looking for people who say, "I'm available. I'm surrendered."

—Sharon Ries

Rahab

A Woman of Courage

by Sharon Ries

The LORD your God, He is God in heaven above and on earth beneath. Now therefore, I beg you, swear to me by the LORD, since I have shown you kindness, that you also will show kindness to my father's house, and give me a true token, and spare my father, my mother, my brothers, my sisters, and all that they have, and deliver our lives from death.
—Joshua 2:11–13

*I*n 2003, the California wildfires raged within thirty yards of our new house. We had sold our old home when a freeway was built nearby, and I wondered, *Is God going to take this new house away?* It is so good to know that even if God takes all that we own, we can look to Him and trust Him because He is in control and He loves us. Our lives belong to Him!

Rahab was a woman who looked to God when destruction was fast approaching. Her story is that of a harlot who came to trust in Jehovah, the God of Israel, and as a result, she found personal deliverance in the midst of the annihilation of the wicked city of Jericho. (This event occurred in approximately 1451 BC.) Later, she married Salmon, who is believed to have been one of the spies in this story. Rahab bore a son by Salmon, bringing her into the ancestral bloodline of King David and Christ Jesus, the Savior of the world.

God is not looking for perfect people to perform His wonders and accomplish His eternal purposes. He is looking for people who say, *I'm available. I'm surrendered.* Sometimes we think we can't give much time to God. But our lives belong to Him twenty-four hours a day whether we are at church, in our neighborhoods, with our children, or at work.

Second Chronicles 16:9 says, *The eyes of the LORD run to and fro throughout the whole earth, to shew himself strong in the behalf of them whose heart is perfect toward him* (KJV)—not those who *are* perfect, but those who have a perfect *heart* towards Him and are loving Him, trusting Him, and depending upon Him in every circumstance, no matter how desperate. The word translated *perfect* in this verse means "complete, friendly, made ready, peaceable, quiet." It describes a person who sits still and knows that God is in control of every situation.

The first part of Rahab's name comes from the name of the Egyptian god, *Ra*, which her people, the Amorites, worshiped. Her name means "insolence, fierceness, broad spaciousness." She was a captive maiden of her gods and of the walls of Jericho. Many of us came from situations that made us feel imprisoned. For years I was held captive to an aggressive husband, and then the Lord delivered me by bringing salvation to him.

Matthew 1:5 records the genealogy of Jesus Christ. It tells us that *Salmon begot Boaz by Rahab.* Boaz was a type of Christ in the book of Ruth. He married Ruth the Moabitess and they begat Obed, whose wife gave birth to Jesse, the father of King David. Jesus came from the line of David. In order for the Jews to accept Jesus as king, He had to be a descendant of David, which He was—physically through Mary and legally through Joseph.

In Joshua 1:2–3, we read that the Lord spoke to Joshua, the son of Nun, saying, *Moses My servant is dead. Now therefore, arise, go over this Jordan, you and all this people, to the land which I am giving to them— the children of Israel. Every place that the sole of your foot will tread upon I have given you.* Moses' call was given to Joshua. How would you like to fulfill someone else's call? Most of us want our own call. Joshua was asked to do exactly what God had commanded Moses to do because Moses, through one act of disobedience, had forfeited his right to see his calling through to the end.

In verse 5, God said, *No man shall be able to stand before you all the days of your life; as I was with Moses, so I will be with you. I will not leave you nor forsake you.* Then, in verses 7–9: *Observe . . . all the law which Moses My servant commanded you. . . . This Book of the Law shall not depart from your mouth, but you shall meditate in it day and night, that you may observe to do according to all that is written in it. For then you will make your way prosperous, and then you will have good success. Have I not commanded you? Be strong and of good courage; do not be afraid, nor be dismayed, for the* LORD *your God is with you wherever you go.*

This is the man, the people, and the God that Rahab had heard about in Jericho.

In chapters 1 and 2, Joshua was commanded by God to cross the Jordan River and take the fortified city of Jericho in the Promised Land. God was about to defeat all their enemies and give His people everything He had promised. God has also promised that we are kingdom children, and that He will defeat our enemies.

Verses 1 and 2 of chapter 2 say, *Now Joshua the son of Nun sent out two men from Acacia Grove to spy secretly, saying, "Go, view the land, especially Jericho." So they went, and came to the house of a harlot named Rahab, and lodged there.* Jericho was the key city in the rich Jordan valley. The surrounding terrain was desolate, dry, and rocky. Travelers would stop in this heavily fortified city for food and refreshment. It was an Amorite civilization, devoid of God and totally given over to immorality, like Las Vegas or San Francisco. One commentator said that they practiced every kind of evil and debased deed in worship of their gods. (Nowadays we don't actually worship statues; some of the gods of our day are pornography and filth.)

By divine decree, God had commanded Joshua to destroy the city and all its inhabitants, including the animals. They were to keep only the silver and gold, which would be deposited into the treasury of the house of God. After this invasion, Jericho was given over to perpetual desolation. I've been there, and it is still desolate. There are some little shops, but tourists don't want to go there because it is so dangerous. The last time our church took a tour group there, a couple of guys with knives tried to persuade some of us to ride their camels. It's a scary place.

One of the gods deified in Jericho was Chemosh, the god of pleasure. Worshipers believed child sacrifices were necessary in order to appease this god. Like many of the women who choose abortion today, the people of Jericho loved pleasure more than they feared God. They were also devoted to the gods Baal and Ashteroth, and engaged in immoral and sensual perversion to please them.

Two spies were sent to Jericho bearing a message of salvation. In the Bible, the number two stands for witnesses. When Jesus sent out the disciples, He sent them out two-by-two, so that they were accountable to each other; and, during the last three-and-a-half years of the Great Tribulation, two Old Testament saints are going to witness and be martyred on the streets of Jerusalem. (Some believe them to be Moses and Elijah.) These two messengers to Jericho are a type of two witnesses going into an immoral place, but they were there to get information.

The Bible offers no excuse for the spies having entered a harlot's house, either in this passage or when the books of the New

Testament refer to Rahab. Inns like Rahab's were the *Travelodges* or the *Motel 6s* of the day, but they also had women. A man could hire a woman and get a room, or he could hire a room and a woman would come knocking at his door—even if he didn't want one.

People may ask, *Why would two believers lodge in a harlot's house?* First, they were not looking for women, but were there to spy on the city. Second, Rahab's house would have provided protection because God's people would not be expected to be found there. Third, the loose talk in such an environment would have enabled them to gather a lot of information necessary for waging warfare against the city.

Joshua 2:15 tells us that her house was on the city wall. In ancient times, thick walls protected cities from invading armies. (Today, a wall obviously wouldn't do any good because wars are waged with airplanes.) Rahab's house was built against the exterior wall near the city gate, and it had a window looking out. This meant Rahab could see who was coming into the city. Her house was actually suspended between thick double walls. Imagine living like that! The Bible indicates that there were stairs or some other means of getting up to the flat roof, which appeared to be a continuation of the wall.

The two spies were on a mission from God and He protected them. Have you ever been on a mission from God? A mission from God can be everything that we do all day. Being a mother or a grandmother is a mission. I pray for our daughter-in-law all the time. She has our little grandbaby, and is pregnant with a second child. God has called her to a great mission in raising two children in these last days. We need to look at everything we do as an assignment from God.

In Psalm 18:36, David said, *Thou hast enlarged my steps under me, that my feet did not slip* (KJV). God sends us on missions, and He guides us if we choose to fear Him and are watchful and attentive to His Word. Psalm 37:23–24 says, *The steps of a good man are ordered by the LORD, and He delights in his way. Though he fall, he shall not be utterly cast down; for the LORD upholds him with His hand.* This promise makes me think of Rahab up on that wall, waiting for God's people who had already wiped out the kings of the Amorites and were on their way to destroy her city. She was suspended there by the hand of God.

The last time I went to Colombia, it was during a very dangerous time. I was with a group of women ministering at women's conferences. We didn't want anyone to know we were Americans, so we dressed like the locals, and as we drove through the cities and towns, we kept our heads down and acted like we were students.

We decided to go to this cute town with a little white Catholic church and a beautiful park. It was close to the mission station in the jungle in an area surrounded by guerillas and mercenaries. Both are equally bad and have been known to kidnap Americans for revenue. We were brave enough to get out of the car and take pictures, and even buy some ice cream. I was hiding my face, when all of a sudden this girl said, *Hello. You're Naomi's daughter.* I thought my heart would faint. I froze, but looked up and saw that she had a big smile on her face. Her parents had known my mother, who had been a missionary in Colombia. It was so neat to see that not only did the enemy not see me, but God had provided a friend of the family to greet me in this little town where we *just happened* to stop. I felt so protected by the Lord. I thought to myself, *God knows I'm here. His presence is with me wherever I go!*

I've been in other places where people would sneer. Others would say, *Thanks for coming,* letting me know that they knew who

I was. One time we drove by a snitch named John. He was the person that called the mercenaries if any Americans were around. As we drove past him, we turned our heads, and he didn't notice us. God protected us. Psalm 37:31 says, *The law of his God is in his heart; none of His steps shall slide.* And Psalm 85:13 says, *Righteousness will go before Him, and shall make His footsteps our pathway.*

Nothing in Rahab's life would point to her engaging in a mission from God. Her name comes from the name of an Egyptian god, but *harlot* comes from the word *porn*. People have tried to say that she was not a harlot because they don't want to accept the fact that Jesus could forgive her sins, and that she could be in His genealogy. We don't know what led her to become a harlot, but her name indicates that she could have been used for sexual rites at the temple. Harlots were usually raped, abused, beaten, and sometimes killed. A harlot is a woman that submits to any man who crosses her threshold for sinful purposes. She sells her body for money, and is a prisoner of sin and a victim of circumstances. These women can be completely given over to wickedness in reaction to the people and circumstances in their lives.

Despite her harlotry, Rahab's character was being formed in the midst of this corrupt and abandoned people. It gives me so much comfort to know that God can reach the most unreachable person. We don't know that anybody was praying for Rahab. She was just looking out her tavern window and listening to stories of what God and His people were doing as they marched towards her city, and she believed in Him.

Joshua 2:2–7 records the scene: *And it was told the king of Jericho, saying, "Behold, men have come here tonight from the children of Israel to search out the country." So the king of Jericho sent to Rahab, saying, "Bring out the men who have come to you, who have entered your house, for they have come to search out all the country." Then the woman took the two men and hid them. So she said, "Yes, the men came to me, but I did not know where they were from. And it happened as the gate was being shut, when it was dark, that the men went out. Where the men went I do not know; pursue them quickly, for you may overtake them." (But she had brought them up to the roof and hidden them with the stalks of flax, which she had laid in order on the roof.) Then the men pursued them by the road to the Jordan, to the fords. And as soon as those who pursued them had gone out, they shut the gate.*

The spies had been seen and the king's men were searching for them. They knew that people went to the inn and that it was right inside the city gate. The gate was shut, and Rahab bravely hid the spies on her roof because they were servants of the Lord, and she truly believed in Jehovah God. Perhaps it is symbolic that she covered them with flax because that same material was used by the Jews to make priestly garments. Like priests, these men brought the message of salvation to Rahab. Next, she implemented warfare strategy by lying to their pursuers. In war, people lie to thwart the enemy. If Rahab had been caught, she would have been killed. The Amorites thought nothing of murdering people; they already sacrificed their own babies to their gods.

When Hebrews chapter 11 lists heroes of the faith, only two women are mentioned: Rahab and Sarah. There were many other women of great faith, but the writer of Hebrews was inspired by the Spirit of God to mention these two. Hebrews 11:31 says, *By faith the harlot Rahab did not perish with those who did not believe, when she received the spies with peace.* The people of Jericho were afraid, but they didn't believe in the God of Israel. People often don't even want to hear. Mormons have come to my front door and I've asked them, *Don't you just want to hear what the Bible says because you may be wrong?* I have studied Mormonism and Jehovah's Witnesses and my husband, Raul, has studied other religions, including Islam. It's good to compare their claims to the Bible in order to find out who is telling the truth. But people frequently put their very lives in danger because they choose to believe a lie and refuse to hear anything else. Rahab was smart. She wanted to know, and therefore she listened when she heard about what God was doing. She could discern the truth from the lie. When you seek for the truth, God will show you the truth.

Rahab's attitude wasn't, *Oh, well, I'm going to side with these guys because they're winning.* No, she was a true believer in God and those spies knew it. Because she dwelt in Israel at the end of her life, other people knew it too.

Rahab received the spies in peace, which means she had peace in her heart. She not only possessed faith in God and His power to be victorious, but she also had a confident assurance that she and her family would be delivered from the impending destruction. God will give us His peace in the midst of the chaotic storms that swirl around us.

New Testament writers identify Rahab as a harlot, continuing to distinguish her by her former life, thereby declaring God's transforming power. Raul always likes to remind people that he was a wicked fighter and a Vietnam veteran because he wants to remind himself of who he is apart from Christ. As Christians, we are forgiven of our sin, and we receive a new life. We can then become puffed up, thinking we've made ourselves into something great. But it's good to remember who we are, where we came from, and what God has done.

Scripture says that Rahab believed by faith. What is faith? Hebrews 11:1 says, *Faith is the substance of things hoped for, the evidence of things not seen.* She was probably thinking, *I need to be with those people who are marching toward us. I'm in the wrong place in this city of Jericho.* That was the evidence, or the assurance in her heart, of things not seen. Although she didn't see what God saw, she heard what everybody was talking about, and she believed.

When Joshua and the nation of Israel came to the Jordan River, it parted for them, and they walked through on dry land. God does those kinds of things in the lives of His people. We don't need to fear the Red Sea—God parted it for Moses and all His people—and we don't need to fear the Jordan.

In fact, when the wildfire was coming toward our house last year, Raul had been watching it move closer and closer all day. Finally he said, *It's Monday night. I have to go speak for Greg Laurie at The Grove* (a concert venue in Anaheim, California, where Greg Laurie held a weekly evangelistic outreach). I protested, *You can't. The fire is going to reach our house while you're there.* He pleaded, *Sharon, I have to go. The service is broadcast on the radio. The firemen will be here, you'll be here, and God will be here. Everything will be fine.* I was on the phone with him until one second before he got up to speak. One last time he asked, *Where's the fire?* I responded, *Right in our backyard.* With that he said, *Gotta go. Bye.* I stood alone with the flames in my backyard. The firemen weren't there, my children weren't there—nobody was there. I thought, *Well, Moses parted the Red Sea,* so I lifted my arms wide and prayed, *God, You are my consuming fire. Consume that fire!*

What happened next was so great. The peace that passes all understanding filled my heart. There was an inferno all around my house and I was holding a hose, wetting little patches here and there. I was the only person in the whole neighborhood with a hose. A fireman came by and said, *If you need to do that for therapy, okay, but it's not going to help. If a fire starts, then you can put water on it.* I thought, *Why does everything have to be therapy?* And, *Don't you want your house wet when there's a fire?* But I turned off the hose.

People were meandering up the street lamenting, *Oh, I don't want my house to burn,* but I had so much peace in my heart. Before Raul left, we had been outside having coffee and watching the fire. The neighbors were asking, *Why are you guys so happy?* We weren't foolish however. I took Raul's computer, our important papers, and five generations of pictures out of the house and put them in my car. Then we waited to see what God would do. He kept the wind going the other way. At two o'clock in the morning, the firemen said the wind would shift toward our house. At one point, the flames, which had been blowing away from the house, appeared to stand straight up, and I thought, *Oh boy, here it comes.* I started praying, *Lord, blow it backwards,* and even though it came extremely close to our house, the wind took it in the opposite direction. God delivered us.

In verses 8–11, Rahab made a declaration that led to her deliverance: *Now before they lay down, she came up to them on the roof, and said to the men: "I know that the LORD has given you the land, that the terror of you has fallen on us, and that all the inhabitants of the land are fainthearted because of you. For we have heard how the LORD dried up the water of the Red Sea for you when you came out of Egypt, and what you did to the two kings of the Amorites who were on the other side of the Jordan, Sihon and Og, whom you utterly destroyed. And as soon as we heard these things, our hearts melted; neither did there remain any more courage in anyone because of you, for the LORD your God, He is God in heaven above and on earth beneath."*

Here we have Rahab's total confession. She admitted that the people in Jericho were afraid: *We are terrorized. We are fearful. God is with you.* Her heart melted along with everyone else's. The inhabitants of the city had all heard, but only Rahab believed. She saw what was happening: these strong, aggressive kings were afraid of the children of Israel who didn't even have weapons because they knew God fought for these invaders. Remarkably, they didn't turn to God; they just waited to be destroyed.

We can be like the children of Israel—not prideful or aggressive, but people who are submissive, surrendered, and obedient to God. Then those around us will literally fear us. I remember sitting in church listening to pastors speak, and I would hide because I thought, *They know what I'm going through.* In reality, God was telling those speakers something that I needed to hear and it was great. We should do what Rahab did. Instead of being fearful of people that speak for God, we should learn from them, and absorb what they are teaching us.

In this story, we see God's divine grace as He called forth His church out of a godless society. He called Rahab out of that society. Because there are people in my family that I love who don't walk with God, it comforts me to know that God can eventually pull them out of our godless society. He pulled Noah out of the flood, and only Noah and eight people were saved; He pulled Lot out of the city of Sodom and Gomorrah; and He's calling us out today.

Matthew 10:32–33 says, *Therefore whoever confesses Me before men, him I will also confess before My Father who is in heaven. But whoever denies Me before men, him I will also deny before My Father who is in heaven.* Imagine Jesus in heaven delighting Himself in the Father, but seeing Rahab and saying, *Look at that woman down there. She's a harlot. She has never been able to believe any man. She has been used and abused, but she's confessing Me. Let's do something really cool and get her out of there.*

The Lord confesses us before the Father. First John 1:9 says, *If we confess our sins, He is faithful and just to forgive us our sins and to cleanse us from all unrighteousness.* Be honest and true before God. First John 4:15 says, *Whoever confesses that Jesus is the Son of God, God abides in him, and he in God.* Think about what that means. We become one with God when we confess Jesus Christ as our Lord. However, be assured that until Satan is thrown into the lake of fire along with death and hell, he will try to get us to deny that Jesus Christ is the Son of God. He wants us to forfeit our trust in God because of the horrible circumstances that might be happening in our lives.

Through her confession, Rahab was completely transformed while living in the midst of an idolatrous nation. God had revealed Himself to her through His acts towards His people, and she believed. She made the Lord her God, her Savior, and her Redeemer. She left the world that held her captive to sin. She confessed a new Lord, and He became her only love and her reason for living. It is so important to see God acting in our lives and to believe.

Rahab's salvation is recorded in verses 12–24: *"Now therefore, I beg you, swear to me by the LORD, since I have shown you kindness, that you also will show kindness to my father's house, and give me a true token, and spare my father, my mother, my brothers, my sisters, and all that they have, and deliver our lives from death."*

So the men answered her, "Our lives for yours, if none of you tell this business of ours. And it shall be, when the LORD has given us the land, that we will deal kindly and truly with you."

Then she let them down by a rope through the window, for her house was on the city wall; she dwelt on the wall. And she said to them, "Get to the mountain, lest the pursuers meet you. Hide there three days, until the pursuers have returned. Afterward you may go your way."

So the men said to her: "We will be blameless of this oath of yours which you have made us swear, unless, when we come into the land, you bind this line of scarlet cord in the window through which you let us down, and unless you bring your father, your mother, your brothers, and all your father's household to your own home. So it shall be that whoever goes outside the doors of your house into the street, his blood shall be on his own head, and we will be guiltless. And whoever is with you in the house, his blood shall be on our head if a hand is laid on him. And if you tell this business of ours, then we will be free from your oath which you made us swear."

Then she said, "According to your words, so be it." And she sent them away, and they departed. And she bound the scarlet cord in the window.

They departed and went to the mountain, and stayed there three days until the pursuers returned. The pursuers sought them all along the way, but did not find them. So the two men returned, descended from the mountain, and crossed over; and they came to Joshua the son of Nun, and told him all that had befallen them. And they said to Joshua, "Truly the LORD has delivered all the land into our hands, for indeed all the inhabitants of the country are fainthearted because of us."

Rahab wanted the spies to give their word in front of the Lord because she believed in Him. In those days, people would give something such as a shoe, a ring, or an earring as a token of their vow's worth. This red token visible from her window was a sign to the godly people and to anybody in the outside world that she believed in the ultimate triumph of Jehovah. She had probably used this cord to let things down through the window and to bring up food and provisions that had been delivered from the market. Can you imagine how that scarlet cord looked? The spies could see the rope, and as they left her house, they said, *Watch for the rope. That's where the woman who believes God lives. We're going to save her out of all the people.* There are types and symbols throughout the Bible and this red cord was symbolic of the saving power of the blood of Jesus extending from heaven to mankind before it was ever shed.

Another symbol of the saving power of the blood of Jesus is found in the story of the exodus from Egypt. After God had sent numerous plagues, and Pharaoh still wouldn't let the people go, God sent the final plague—the destruction of the firstborn of every household in Egypt. Moses commanded the Hebrews to put blood from an unblemished lamb on the doorposts and lintels of their houses. When the angel of death saw the red mark, he would pass over that house.

The red cord symbolized redemption for the spies. By it, these messengers of the Lord escaped from a wicked city where they could have been destroyed. Rahab sent their pursuers toward the Jordan River, but she sent the spies to the mountains. In return, they advised her to keep all of her family inside the house. They told her to bind the scarlet cord in the window so that they would know which house was hers when they came back to attack the city.

Rahab could have said, *I don't want to use a scarlet cord. I want to use a white one or some other sign.* She didn't argue, but obeyed in those little things, and that scarlet cord became a very significant symbol. It was salvation for her and her family from the corrupt city that had violated her and held her captive her entire life. It was also a statement to the world similar to what Joshua said at the end of the book: *As for me and my house, we will serve the LORD* (24:15). Each family member had to make a decision to stay in that house.

I love Rahab because she was not consumed with self. She wanted to extend salvation to her father, her brothers, and her sisters. Scripture doesn't say that they believed, but she was extending salvation to them, and perhaps hoping they would believe once they were safe and in the midst of these people. We too can extend the cord of salvation to our families that they might be delivered from the world. Recently I was thinking, *Can anybody tell that Christians live in my house?* The answer is yes. I have a flag that says, *God Bless America*, and a steppingstone that says, *Give thanks to the Lord for He is good.* You can't come into the house without reading it.

We have those visible signs, but our lives should testify that we are Christians as well. On the night of the fire, we were just sitting outside, drinking our coffee, waiting on the Lord to see what He would do, and that caused our neighbors to inquire about our faith.

First John 1:7 says, *If we walk in the light as He is in the light, we have fellowship with one another, and the blood of Jesus Christ His Son cleanses us from all sin.* *All* means past, present, and future sin. Hebrews 9:22 says, *Without [the] shedding of blood, there is no remission [of sin].* Jesus Christ is always in search of sinners. He sought them out when He walked on the dirt roads of the world and He continues to search them out today. He is not willing that any soul should perish.

James 2:25 says, *Likewise, was not Rahab the harlot also justified by works when she received the messengers and sent them out another way?* *Justified* means "just as if she had never sinned." The blood of Jesus Christ justifies and cleanses us. He sees us as if we had never sinned. Rahab was justified. In Joshua chapter 6, we see her new status. Joshua came, God parted the Jordan, and all the people walked through on dry land. They built an altar of rocks, and God told them that this would be a sign to their children that He had not only parted the Red Sea for His people, but also that He had parted the Jordan so they could cross over and take the Promised Land (Joshua chapter 4). And then God commanded Joshua to walk around Jericho once a day for six days with the priests bearing the Ark and blowing rams' horns. On the seventh day, they walked around Jericho seven times. Imagine Rahab and her family looking out her window: Someone asks, *What are they doing?* Rahab answers, *They're walking around. Nothing is happening.* Someone else says, *What are they doing now?* She responds, *They're walking around again, and still nothing happened.* But then on the seventh day, which is the number of perfection, they marched around the city seven times, blew their horns, and the walls fell down. What an awesome story!

Chapter 6, verse 17 reads, *Now the city shall be doomed by the LORD to destruction, it and all who are in it. Only Rahab the harlot shall live, she and all who are with her in the house, because she hid the messengers.* What a little thing for her to do, and yet it was great in the eyes of the Lord.

Verses 20–24 describe the invasion: *The wall fell down flat. . . . And they utterly destroyed all that was in the city. . . . But Joshua had said to the two men who had spied out the country, "Go into the harlot's house, and from there bring out the woman and all that she has, as you swore to her." And the young men who had been spies went in and brought out Rahab, her father, her mother, her brothers, and all that she had. So they brought out all her relatives and left them outside the camp of Israel. But they burned the city and all that was in it with fire. Only the silver and gold, and the vessels of bronze and iron, they put into the treasury of the house of the LORD.*

Verse 25 concludes, *And Joshua spared Rahab the harlot, her father's household, and all that she had. So she dwells in Israel to this day, because she hid the messengers whom Joshua sent to spy out Jericho.*

Matthew says that Salmon, a prince in the tribe of Judah, married her. He was an honorable man. Rahab had lived a life of dishonor with dishonorable people, but she chose the God who is above all gods. He recompensed her by giving her physical and spiritual life as well as the true love of an honorable man. God's eternal and perfect plan was worked through a woman of ill repute who entrusted her life to Him. Her eternal Husband gave her purity and an eternal purpose. Instead of being called Rahab the harlot of Jericho, she became Rahab the harlot in the line of Jesus.

Her life should make us ponder what God could do if we would put our trust in Him and totally turn our lives over to Him. When we make Him Lord of our lives, we become one with Him and become a part of His plans. Seek first the kingdom of God and His righteousness and everything else will be added unto you. You can trust and depend upon Him to take care of you, your family, and all that concerns you. When you believe on the Lord Jesus Christ, your sins will be washed away by the blood of the Lamb of God who takes away the sins of the world. As with the scarlet cord, your life will testify that you belong to Jesus, and it will offer the way of salvation to those who don't believe!

Reflections

1. Take this time and meditate on the life of Rahab.
2. What lessons on faith do you learn from her life?
3. The scarlet cord, a symbol of the blood of Christ, was hung in Rahab's window. As a result, she and her household were spared. How does her act of faith encourage you to trust in God's grace, forgiveness, and salvation?
4. In what area do you need to trust in God's grace, forgiveness, or salvation?
5. Take hold of the promise of 1 John 1:9 and give thanks for His cleansing power.

About the Author

Sharon Ries lived in South America with her missionary parents until she was thirteen years old. During Sharon's second year in college, she married Raul A. Ries, a non-believer Marine stationed in Vietnam. After four years in an abusive marriage, Sharon took Raul to Calvary Chapel Costa Mesa during the Jesus Movement. Receiving Christ while listening to Pastor Chuck Smith, Raul ended a life of anger and violence. Today Raul is the senior pastor of Calvary Chapel Golden Springs in Diamond Bar, California, and evangelist of *Somebody Loves You* crusades.

Sharon is a Bible teacher and missionary who has a passion for the Word of God and for souls. She is on the planning boards for women's ministries in South America, Calvary Chapel pastors' wives retreats, and Latin Ladies Conferences in the United States. The story of her life has been documented in the book and film, *From Fury to Freedom*, *Always* by Focus on the Family, and Sharon's own book *My Husband, My Maker*.

If you walk around with a scowl on your face all the time, it says your God must be angry or mean. But if joy lights up your face, it reveals internal peace and visibly demonstrates that God is loving and compassionate.

—Jean McClure

Euodia and Syntyche

Two Women of Conflict

by Jean McClure

—∞∞∞—

Therefore, my beloved and longed-for brethren, my joy and crown, so stand fast in the Lord, beloved. I implore Euodia and I implore Syntyche to be of the same mind in the Lord. And I urge you also, true companion, help these women who labored with me in the gospel.
—Philippians 4:1–3

These two women, Euodia and Syntyche, remind me of Lucy and Ethel from the *I Love Lucy* show because Lucy and Ethel were always arguing about something. Euodia and Syntyche weren't just doing slapstick on a television sitcom though. They were struggling to get along with each other even though they seemed to be godly Christian women. They had worked with Paul, but their conflict became so public that he had to rebuke them in this little epistle, which means two thousand years later we still know that they did not get along. How embarrassing their arrival in heaven must have been! I bet they wished they had worked out their disagreements on earth, and perhaps they did after this letter was circulated and everyone else in the vicinity learned about their conflict. Sometimes fighting is just not worth the embarrassment and humiliation. I love the fact that

God, in His Word, reveals other people's weaknesses and strengths so that we can learn from them.

Have you ever fought with someone? Romans 12:18 tells us, *If it is possible, as much as depends on you, live peaceably with all men.* This Scripture has always been a comfort to me because the phrase *If it is possible* lets me know that God acknowledges it isn't always possible. We are going to have conflicts. One commentary says that Paul had to rebuke these women publicly because their conflict had escalated to the point of causing division in the church at Philippi.

I love Philippians 4:1–3 because I like peacefulness. I'm the kind of person who says, *Come on, let's have a good time. Don't be sad. Don't be mad at anybody. Life is too short!* Unfortunately, conflict impacts us in every area of life, whether it's at work, with our children, in our marriage, or with friends and relatives. It's not always easy to get along because God gives each of us different personalities, but His Word instructs us how to live peaceably with one another. It provides examples, promises, and commands on dealing with problems in a godly manner. Our tendency to disagree and then cast blame on someone else started in the garden of Eden. Adam said, *Lord, it was the woman that You made. You created Eve and gave her to me. I didn't even know to ask for her. She gave me the fruit, so deal with her* (see Genesis 3). He passed the buck. The Lord then confronted Eve, and she said, *The serpent deceived me.* We've learned well how to blame our problems on other people. When my three sons were little, the two older ones would blame their mischief on the youngest because they could talk and he couldn't. One day, the youngest had a little problem in his diapers. I said, *What have you done?* To my amazement, he said his older brother did it. They had taught him well! It's the fallen nature of man to pass the buck.

Some years ago, my husband Don went to Pastor Chuck Smith and said, *Chuck, send me someplace that no one else wants to go.* He had been ministering in Redlands, California, where we had started a church that was going well. He'd been there eleven years and he felt like the Lord was saying it was time for him to move on. He told Chuck, *I need a challenge. I don't want to end up like a surgeon who got into medicine to repair bodies on the frontlines of the battlefield, but ended up performing face lifts in Palm Springs.* He said, *I really want to go to the frontlines, Chuck.*

That very week a pastor from a denominational church in San Jose, California, had said to Chuck, *I'm leaving my church. It's a mess—8.5 million dollars in debt—and if Calvary Chapel wants it, it's yours.* As Don was speaking, Chuck replayed this conversation in his mind. With an unforgettable smile on his face, Chuck said, *Have I got a challenge for you!* As he explained the situation, Don retreated, *Go ahead and ask Jon Courson to take that church.* (Jon had grown up there and was considering taking the pastorate.)

All the way home, the Lord convicted Don, saying, *You asked Me where to go and I told Chuck to tell you and you're not listening.* Don argued, *But God, this isn't exactly what I had in mind when I was thinking about a challenge.* When he got home, he called Chuck and told him he would take the church if Jon didn't want it. Then Jon Courson called and said, *I don't like three-piece suits or money problems. I think this church is perfect for Don, and we're praying for you guys.* Some years later, I was sitting in that church on a Sunday morning and I saw Jon and Tammy Courson. They were on vacation and wanted to see how things were going. I sat next to them and whispered, *Aren't you glad you didn't take it?* Actually, the church was doing well by that time, but the situation had gotten so bad before we arrived that they were taking three offerings at each service. The secretary recognized a ring that we found in the office and said, *That gal's husband had an affair and she put it in the offering plate.*

It was awful. There were two camps and people were fighting with one another in the foyer. One day, Kay Smith called me and said, *Jean, just love those people. Don't take sides. Don't offer your opinion. Just love them and be quiet. In six months, they'll trust you.* That was the best advice. The congregation did begin to trust us because we were all they had left!

One morning as Don was preaching, he said, *I'm not going to plead for money in this church.* The people were so relieved that they clapped. The Lord began to work by miraculously supplying money to pay the bills. God met them in their need. Those that loved the Lord stayed, and those that were a wreck over the situation left. I found that if I would just love them, they would begin to love each other. That's what getting along is all about: loving one another.

Immediately preceding Paul's rebuke to Euodia and Syntyche, he wrote, *Therefore, my beloved and longed-for brethren, my joy and my crown, so stand fast in the Lord, beloved* (verse 1). We should be united, joyful, and in prayer. This lays out a principle for how Christians can get along. First, we need to be united and joyful because when people see unified, joyful Christians, it's a great testimony. If you walk around with a scowl on your face all the time, it says your God must be angry or mean. But if joy lights up your face, it reveals internal peace and visibly demonstrates that God is loving and compassionate.

Second, be in prayer because that's how problems are solved. Prayer is the place where our minds can meet. In high school, I read something in a book by a missionary to China that said, *Loving folks is the only way to win them.* That taught me to take people I struggled with to the Lord in prayer. When I pray for people, God lets me see them more clearly and He gives me compassion and love for them. You can work things out that way. If you're in prayer, you'll be more apt to be joyful, and then you'll be more likely to be united.

In Genesis chapter 13, we read about a family dispute that Abraham had to settle with his nephew, Lot. Theirs was a godly family and yet they were having problems. The story begins as follows:

Lot also, who went with Abram, had flocks and herds and tents. Now the land was not able to support them, that they might dwell together, for their possessions were so great that they could not dwell together. And there was strife between the herdsmen of Abram's livestock and the herdsmen of Lot's livestock. The Canaanites and the Perizzites then dwelt in the land.

So Abram said to Lot, "Please let there be no strife between you and me, and between my herdsmen and your herdsmen; for we are brethren. Is not the whole land before you? Please separate from me. If you take the left, then I will go to the right, or, if you go to the right, then I will go to the left."

And Lot lifted his eyes and saw all the plain of Jordan, that it was well watered everywhere (before the LORD destroyed Sodom and Gomorrah) like the garden of the LORD, like the land of Egypt as you go toward Zoar. Then Lot chose for himself all the plain of Jordan, and Lot journeyed east. And they separated from each other. Abram dwelt in the land of Canaan, and Lot dwelt in the cities of the plain and pitched his tent even as far as Sodom. But the men of Sodom were exceedingly wicked and sinful against the LORD (verses 5–13).

Abraham (whose pre-covenant name was Abram) and Lot were ranchers who had amassed a lot of cattle and wealth between them, and their herdsmen were fighting over the land. When the American pioneers came west, there were wars between shepherds and cattlemen because the sheep would destroy the grass by eating it all the way down to the roots, and then the ranchers' cattle wouldn't have food. Abraham and Lot's situation was similar. There wasn't enough room on the land for everyone, so they needed to separate. Abraham, being the patriarch of the family and a godly man, settled the dispute in such a beautiful, peaceful way. He gave Lot what he wanted, saying, *You choose and I'll take the opposite, and that's okay with me.* Lot's choice tells us much about him. He looked up and saw the best land, the well-watered land, and said, *I'll take that.* He was very selfish.

In the children's book *Charlotte's Web*, a rat named Templeton was given the job of collecting scraps of paper with words on them for the spider, Charlotte, to weave into her web. Every time Templeton was sent to the dump, he would ask, *What's in it for me?*[1] What a beautiful sentence of selfishness: *What's in it for me?* We live in a generation of completely selfish people. Everybody says, *I have rights; it's all about me; if it makes me feel good, I'm going to do it, and I don't care what you think.* Generosity has gone out the window and selfishness has come in. Satan was a gorgeous angel in heaven who said, *I will be like the Most High God.* He is the ultimate portrait of narcissism and selfishness. In contrast is the crucified Christ—the ultimate picture of total unselfishness and sacrifice.

Lot made a decision that seemed very logical to him: *My animals will eat because there's water and green grass on the land I'm choosing,* but Sodom was waiting for him. Selfishness always leads to loss and misery. In verse 18, we read that *Abram moved his tent, and went and dwelt by the terebinth trees of Mamre, which are in Hebron, and built an altar there to the Lord.* Mamre means "strength" and Hebron means "fellowship." This reveals another contrast between Lot and Abraham. Abraham moved towards strength and fellowship, while Lot moved closer and closer to the gates of Sodom until he moved right in and became one of the elders in the city. Abraham generously gave Lot the best land. If we deny ourselves for the sake of peace like Abraham did, the Lord will more than make it up to us.

---

[1] White, E. B. *Charlotte's Web.* New York: Harper Trophy, 1952.

One of my favorite Scriptures, Matthew 5:9, says, *Blessed are the peacemakers, for they shall be called sons of God.* Abraham became a son and friend of God. He was a peacemaker. As soon as he had given Lot the best land and was preparing to move his tents and family, the Lord declared, *Abram, I've got some good news for you.* God saw that Abraham had surrendered himself, and He more than made it up to him with this promise: *Lift your eyes now and look from the place where you are—northward, southward, eastward, and westward; for all the land which you see I give to you and your descendants forever* (Genesis 13:14–15). Then He said, *I will make your descendants as the dust of the earth; so that if a man could number the dust of the earth, then your descendants also could be numbered. Arise, walk in the land through its length and its width, for I give it to you* (verses 16–17). God always keeps His promises.

Today Abraham's descendants, the Jews, live in the very land God promised to him. Isn't that a beautiful picture of the returns we receive when we surrender to the Lord? Look at the returns on Lot's selfishness. He ended up with nothing. His wife became a pillar of salt and his name is forever stained with shame.

Often in disagreements, we think we're right, and the other person thinks they're right. So how do we solve the problem? We ask the Lord for wisdom and He'll give it abundantly. When there's a conflict between two people, somebody always has to die to self. We learn in marriage that if there is conflict, someone has to give in. Men and women of God learn to surrender because it resolves disagreements and leads to holiness and a righteous life.

King Solomon was asked to resolve a problem between two women who were fighting over a baby (1 Kings 3). One woman's baby had died, and she claimed that the living baby was hers. Solomon said, *Let's cut the baby in half and you can each have a piece.* He had asked God for wisdom and God gave him great wisdom. The real mother cried out, *Let the other woman have the baby* because she didn't want her child to die. She was willing to surrender out of love. We must surrender out of love for one another.

Peace often requires self-sacrifice. Charles Spurgeon said, *If we desire closer communion with God, we must keep closer to the ways of peace.*[2] Jesus is the great example who gave Himself to bring us peace. Isaiah 52:14 says that He was marred more than any man. When He was treated so abominably on the cross, He said, *Father, forgive them, for they do not know what they do* (Luke 23:34). He had no fault in Him and yet He forgave.

Peacemakers are wise people. Think of Abigail's wisdom. Part of her life story is recorded in 1 Samuel 25:1–42. Abigail's husband, Nabal, rudely refused to provide food for David and his hungry soldiers, even though David's army had protected Nabal's herdsmen in the wilderness. David was so filled with righteous indignation that he intended to kill Nabal's entire household, but Abigail did three wise things to avert disaster. First, she packed raisin cakes and other goodies on donkeys and rode to meet David. How wise Abigail was to know that these men were hungry and grouchy. My mother always said not to talk to your husband about the problems of the day until after he's had dessert because he'll have a whole different attitude after he's eaten. Abigail brought David an offering.

Second, she went right up to him and immediately said, *Please forgive us and don't pay any attention to my husband because he is foolish.* That's a wonderful principle for getting along. People can't fight with you when you ask for their forgiveness, even if you're not wrong. One of my sweet daughters-in-law reminded me of that recently. This person was grappling with a big problem and felt I had neglected her. My daughter-in-law called and said, *Just tell her you're sorry. That's all you have to say. Then listen to her talk about her problems.* I did and it worked

---

[2] Spurgeon, C. H. *Faith's Checkbook.* Chicago: Moody Press, 2004.

like a charm. When I apologized, the person said, *I accept your apology*, and then we were fine. I have found that asking for forgiveness heals a multitude of sins.

Third, Abigail appealed to David's integrity. She fed him, asked for forgiveness, and then appealed to his walk with God, saying, *David, if you don't kill all the men in my family today, you will be so grateful later because when you are king, you'll look back on this day and not be ashamed of your behavior.* He praised her and took her advice.

God protected Abigail from her ungodly husband. He failed in this chance to be kind and generous, so the Lord removed him by causing him to drop dead. It turned out pretty well for her, though, because David sent for her and married her. I don't know how great it was to be his wife, but he did have a heart after God. The principles in this story are so important in learning how to get along. Abigail asked for wisdom and she received it. When we ask the Lord for wisdom, He will help us.

Someone once shared a helpful communication skill with me. When a person says something hurtful to you and you don't understand, respond by saying, *What I hear you saying is this*, and then repeat what you heard. That gives them an opportunity to say, *No, that's not how I meant it*, or, if you heard them correctly, you can then deal with the problem.

Sometimes our conflicts can be used of the Lord. Paul and Barnabas had a disagreement that split up their missionary team. Afterwards, however, they became two missionary teams, which doubled their effectiveness. Joseph, the son of Jacob, definitely had good reasons to be angry with his brothers, yet because he didn't grow bitter and always sought the Lord, God was able to use his situation to save a whole area of the world from starvation.

Peacemakers are kind. I cannot imagine the Lord ever being rude. Manners, kindness, and love are vitally important. We can easily get to the end of our own sweetness, but we'll never get to the end of God's sweetness. You might say, *Jean, that's great. I'm glad we're supposed to get along. But you don't know my relative or friend. You don't know what I've gone through with my neighbor.* Perhaps you are getting to the end of your own sweetness. If you draw on the Holy Spirit, He'll fill you with God's sweetness and help you work it out. He knows we're not perfect. He knows we can't do anything in our own strength. Make a decision to follow the Lord's example. God is kind and gracious to us, so we need to be kind and gracious to others.

Love is the answer to all things. It calms the agitated heart. Romans 13:9 says, *You shall love your neighbor as yourself.* Love does no harm to neighbors. In Philippians 4:1, Paul calls these brethren *my beloved, my joy and crown*, and says he longs for them. What a loving approach and what a great example of how we're to love one another.

When I was a young mother disciplining my first child, my mom said, *Honey, choose your battles.* I found in raising three boys that it was important to choose my battles. Some things are not worth battling over, but there are others that we are allowed to fight over as Christians—such as the integrity of the Word of God, salvation by grace, and our faith in Jesus Christ. Those are issues for which saints have been martyred. Nothing of self is worth fighting for, only the things of the cross.

Peacemakers help others. In the end, Paul appeals to the church at Philippi to help Euodia and Syntyche get along. That's what the body of Christ is all about. When there's a rift, when there are struggles amongst friends, maybe you can see the picture better from outside the circle and the Lord would have you enter in to help. How wonderful it is to be a peacemaker.

Matthew 5:44 says, *Love your enemies . . . and pray for those who spitefully use you.* I know from my own life just how difficult it can be to obey this verse. I want to share a confession and it isn't a pretty picture. I'm ashamed to reveal it, but it's true. Many years ago, Don and I had difficulty getting along with a particular family. One day I went to Don's office and the husband was yelling at him in front of his staff. From time to time, this man's wife would write to Don saying that the Lord had told her we were supposed to leave town and leave the church. As these issues continued to confront us, I grew to dislike this family more and more.

I would get so upset with them because my feelings were hurt. Others who knew what was going on were upset too. One day I got a phone call from my son and he said, *You know what Mom? You have to work it out with these people.* So I called Don who was speaking on the East Coast and told him about the latest offense. I complained, *I feel so awful and I'm so mad and . . .* Don stopped me and said, *I am three thousand miles away from home and I cannot help you with this right now.* Normally he would have said, *Let's pray,* or, *We'll work it out when I get home,* but he couldn't address the problem right then. Realizing I was all alone with this situation, I began to walk through the house weeping. I confessed, *Lord, I really hate these people. They've caused nothing but havoc.* I don't say that lightly because I think it is abominable to say you hate anybody. But I had really gone the gamut with them.

The Lord responded, *Good. Now that we have everything out in the open, let's call this what it is: sin. You can't hate anybody.* I knew He was right because, of course, He's always right. But I like to have these little discussions with Him. I finally said, *Lord, I can forgive them if You help me.* But I was afraid that if I forgave them, they would just do something else that would bring the past rolling back into my mind again. The Lord gave me this assurance: *Jean, if you will keep your mouth closed, I will take care of your heart.* What a novel idea! I thought, *That's good.*

I had a girlfriend that knew about the whole situation, and I told her what the Lord had said. She looked at me quizzically and asked, *Can you do it?* I said, *With everything in me, I'm going to try.* After that, when I would receive negative letters or other incidents would happen, and people would ask questions about the situation, I would respond, *I can't talk about it.* The Lord helped me keep my mouth shut, which was a total miracle.

That Christmas I decided to send a note telling these people that I was praying for their son who was serving overseas in a time of war. The next thing I knew, I got one back. Months later, I received a phone call and a dinner invitation. They apologized and we're friends to this day. The Lord completely healed the whole situation.

It was a great lesson for me to learn that if we will not talk about our conflicts with others, God will take care of them. Remember, God is still on the throne. We're not going to get along with every-body, and it's okay to have disagreements. The *most* important thing is that we love one another. Jesus said, *By this all will know that you are My disciples, if you have love for one another* (John 13:35).

Perhaps you are struggling with someone in your life right now. First, ask the Lord for wisdom; second, ask Him to help you forgive; and third, let His Spirit pour His love into your heart for that person. Watch the Lord begin to heal the conflict. Because we are living in the last days before His return, there is no time to fight with one another. Our battle should be for the souls of those who are lost. May the Lord constantly remind us to love one another and to be of one mind in Him.

Reflections

1. Stop and consider the subject of conflict as addressed in this message.

2. What spiritual lessons stand out from the many examples given?

3. How do you respond when there is conflict in your life?

4. What principles have you learned here that will encourage you to become a peacemaker?

5. Perhaps you are struggling with someone in your life right now. Take a moment to bring that situation before the Lord. First, ask Him for wisdom; second, ask Him to help you forgive; and third, let His Spirit pour His love into your heart for that person.

About the Author

Jean McClure was raised in a Christian home and gave her heart to Christ as a young girl. She spent her high school years at a Christian boarding school in Florida, and married her husband Don when they were college seniors. They spent one year at Capernwray Bible School in England before Don began serving in various pastoral and administrative positions throughout the Calvary Chapel movement. Jean has been a pastor's wife for over thirty years and is a popular retreat and conference speaker. She and Don have three grown sons and six grandchildren.

May our goal in life be to whole-heartedly follow and please the One who created us for His own pleasure and glory. If we make it our aim to be well-pleasing to Him, He will take care of our legacy to the world.

—Jan Vance

Miriam

A Woman of Strength and Weakness

by Jan Vance

Then his sister said to Pharaoh's daughter, "Shall I go and call a
nurse for you from the Hebrew women, that she may nurse the
child for you?" And Pharaoh's daughter said to her, "Go." So
the maiden went and called the child's mother. The Pharaoh's
daughter said to her, "Take this child away and nurse him for
me, and I will give you your wages."
—Exodus 2:7–9

Perhaps one of the most challenging and important lessons we can learn in life is the pursuit of God's will rather than our own. A close look at Miriam, a woman of God used mightily by Him, reveals the key *do's* and *don'ts* to living lives that are pleasing to the Lord.

The scriptural portrait of Miriam's life is painted in three scenes: Scene one depicts Miriam's person and purpose, and how God used a young girl to implement His plan. Scene two reveals Miriam's position and her praise and worship of God. His call upon her life gets the spotlight in this scene. Scene three shows Miriam's pride and its penalty, and provides a glimpse of how God deals with leaders that choose to manifest self rather than obey Him.

God desired to have a people set apart for Himself. He called Abraham out of Ur and into Canaan. Then Abraham's son Isaac and grandson Jacob were born. Jacob, through Leah, Rachel, and their handmaidens fathered twelve sons from whom the twelve tribes of Israel would descend. One of those sons, Joseph, was sold into Egyptian slavery by his jealous brothers. While in Egypt, Joseph's integrity and his determination to live a life pleasing to God elevated him to a position of responsibility; but after a time he was falsely accused and imprisoned. Even in prison God gave him favor with his captors. His integrity and ability to interpret dreams came to the pharaoh's attention, and he promoted Joseph to the position of prime minister over the nation. When famine struck, Joseph's brothers came to Egypt to buy food and the family was reunited.

In those days, because of all Joseph had done for the nation, Egypt welcomed the people of Israel. But then Joseph, his brothers, and their entire generation died. A new king came into power that knew nothing about Joseph, and the Egyptian people forgot all about the favor they had enjoyed by having God's people living among them. They began to discriminate against the people of Israel and forced them into slave labor. Circumstances became very difficult for the Jews, but God continued to bless them until they became more numerous than the Egyptians who enslaved them. Fear of this great multitude led the new king to order the Hebrew midwives to kill the newborn male children. The midwives let them live because they feared God more than they feared the king's edict. Next, the king enlisted the help of the Egyptian people and commanded that every newborn Hebrew male child be thrown into the Nile River.

It was into these circumstances that Moses was born, and it is here that Miriam is introduced into one of the most familiar stories of the Old Testament. Many of us grew up in Sunday school hearing the story of baby Moses floating along the Nile River in a basket.

The opening scene is recorded in Exodus 2:1–10: *And a man of the house of Levi went and took as a wife a daughter of Levi. So the woman conceived and bore a son. And when she saw that he was a beautiful child, she hid him three months. But when she could no longer hide him, she took an ark of bulrushes for him, daubed it with asphalt and pitch, put the child in it, and laid it in the reeds by the river's bank. And his sister stood afar off, to know what would be done to him.*

Then the daughter of Pharaoh came down to bathe at the river. And her maidens walked along the riverside; and when she saw the ark among the reeds, she sent her maid to get it. And when she opened it, she saw the child, and behold, the baby wept. So she had compassion on him, and said, "This is one of the Hebrew's children."

Then his sister said to Pharaoh's daughter, "Shall I go and call a nurse for you from the Hebrew women, that she may nurse the child for you?" And Pharaoh's daughter said to her, "Go." So the maiden went and called the child's mother. The Pharaoh's daughter said to her, "Take this child away and nurse him for me, and I will give you your wages."

So the woman took the child and nursed him. And the child grew, and she brought him to Pharaoh's daughter, and he became her son. So she called his name Moses, saying, "Because I drew him out of the water."

Miriam's person and purpose are revealed in this scene. God had His hand upon this young girl's life from early childhood. We know from the story that some years before the king issued his edict to destroy the Hebrew children, a man named Amram of the tribe of Levi married his kinswoman, Jochebed, and they had two children. Miriam, the oldest, was probably born soon after their marriage, and Aaron was three years old at the time of Moses' birth. It's uncertain exactly how old Miriam was when Moses was born. Estimates range from seven to thirteen years old, but the consensus seems to be that she was somewhere between twelve and thirteen years of age.

Because Miriam was on the verge of her teenage years, she would have had a great deal of responsibility in caring for her two younger brothers, and particularly for baby Moses. Aaron was only three, and therefore would have been pretty clueless as to what was going on around him. But Miriam, who was obviously intelligent and very discerning for her age, must have been deeply affected by the king's decree. She was at that ripe, tender age when a mother's heart begins to bud forth in a teenage girl.

Pharaoh had probably succeeded in doing away with many of the Hebrew babies, or else Moses' parents would not have gone to such drastic measures in order to save him. In Hebrews 11:23, we read that it was by faith that Moses' parents hid him, not fearing the consequences of the king's edict. Since they had faith, we can assume that they were seeking God for His wisdom about what to do in this situation. In faith, Jochebed prepared an ark (a basket capable of floating) from bulrushes. She set her child in the river and entrusted him to God's keeping. That had to be very difficult. Exodus 2:3 tells us that she didn't set him adrift to float, but rather placed him among the reeds at the river's edge, possibly so it would appear that he had floated to shore.

Verse 4 tells us that Miriam stood *afar off*, or at a distance, to see what would happen to Moses. Perhaps Jochebed couldn't bear to watch what might happen to her baby, or she may have thought that her own appearance nearby would be too conspicuous and therefore asked Miriam to wait and watch. It also could have been Miriam's own idea. In any case, it was dangerous for Miriam because if she had been found out, she and her family probably would have incurred the wrath of the king.

As Miriam peered through the reeds, Pharaoh's daughter sent her maid to fetch the basket. When she opened it, the baby wept, and she had compassion on him. And then, without giving away her relationship with the baby either by word or look, Miriam approached Pharaoh's daughter and offered to find a nurse for the child. She arranged for their own mother to care for him at home. Her quick thinking not only saved Moses' life, but the baby was returned to the arms of his mother, and Pharaoh's daughter actually offered to pay Jochebed to nurse her own child! Only God could do something that wonderful.

Miriam's courage at such an early age indicated the kind of woman she would become. Even when she was young, God's hand was upon her and she was His instrument. How did Miriam learn to be so faithful, responsible, and courageous? She learned those traits from her mother, whose name *Jochebed* means "glory of Jehovah" or "Jehovah is her glory." Jochebed is the first person in Scripture whose name is linked to Jehovah God. She taught Miriam and because she was allowed to nurse the baby Moses for a span of about one thousand days, she had the opportunity to teach him in the ways of God. Miriam most likely played a large role in Moses' early development as well.

There are several life lessons that we can learn from Miriam's early childhood. First, when you reach the limits of your own ability, commit yourself into God's keeping, and wait to see what He will do on your behalf. Perhaps right now you are at the limit of what you can do in a particular situation. You don't know what to do next or where to go. Entrust yourself into God's keeping, and watch what He will do on your behalf.

The second lesson is that God, in His providence, is able to move the hearts of men, women, and children, including a princess, and as Scripture tells us, even a king. The heart of a king will change as easily as the direction of a watercourse in God's hand. If you're having a difficult time right now because someone in authority over you has made your life uncomfortable, then pray for God's grace to bear it, or pray that He will change that person's heart. He is watching and listening, waiting for you to come and ask Him.

The third lesson we can glean from Miriam's early life is that God is able to exceed our expectations when we put our faith and trust in Him. I am sure that neither Jochebed nor Miriam ever dreamed that Moses would be returned to their care and keeping. They were hoping beyond hope that his life would be spared, but

God exceeded their expectations. It is so like the Lord to surprise us when we least expect it.

What are you hoping for right now? What is the desire of your heart? The key is to place your faith and trust in God, and He will do abundantly above all that you can ask or think according to His power (Ephesians 3:20). Psalm 36 says that God's unfailing love is as vast as the heavens and His faithfulness reaches beyond the clouds. It also says that He gives not from the abundance of someone else's house, but from His own house. He lets us drink from His rivers of delight, and He pours out immeasurable, abundant blessing.

After Miriam's role in the deliverance of baby Moses, we hear nothing about her life until after the Jews leave Egypt. However, their history provides a pretty clear picture of what Miriam's upbringing must have been like. She lived in the midst of great poverty and prejudice. Being slaves to the Egyptians, she and her family were viewed as mere property. They were forced into hard labor, and she no doubt experienced some extreme working conditions and witnessed a great deal of injustice. She would have learned to show compassion to those who were suffering but had no voice to complain. Knowing her character, we can assume that she reached out to help as many people as she could, and we can conclude that her character was forged and molded in the fires of adversity.

If you or I are ever tempted to think we are exempt from serving God because we've had a hard time growing up, then we need to remember Miriam. She must have overcome tremendous personal hardship to minister to those around her. From an early age, she was thrust into the limelight and entrusted with a great deal of responsibility and leadership. No doubt, by the time she was grown, she had earned the respect of her entire nation. There is no evidence that Miriam ever married, although some historians believe that she became the wife of Hur, one of Moses' right hand men and an early judge among the people. By all scriptural accounts, it seems that

Miriam remained single, dedicating her life to serving God and His people.

In scene two, Miriam's position of responsibility and her praise of God in that position take center stage. Miriam is first introduced by name in Exodus 15:20 where she is described as Aaron's sister and also as a prophetess. Prophetess is a term that is used only a handful of times in Scripture. It is the Hebrew word *nebiy'ah*, which is the feminine form of the word *prophet*. It means "a speaker of oracles" or "one who speaks not in her own words, but those which she has received from God."

By now, Miriam had not only earned the respect of her own people, but she had also received the call of God upon her life as a leader. Two other passages in Scripture give proof of her position. First, in 1 Chronicles 6:3, she is listed along with Moses and Aaron as children of Amram. It was very rare for a woman to be included in a family genealogy unless she was very prominent and well-known. Her inclusion indicates her significance in the life of Israel. The second proof is found in Micah 6:4 when God said, *I sent before you Moses, Aaron, and Miriam*. The word *sent* in this verse indicates a formal calling from God. In other words, we have it on the basis of Scripture that Miriam was sent out as a leader in the same sense that Moses and Aaron were sent. They fulfilled different roles, but had received the same calling. They did not appoint themselves, but were all uniquely and specifically chosen by God. We are going to see later how important this fact is in God's judgment of Miriam's pride.

We know that Miriam's family was separated while Moses lived as the adopted son of Pharaoh's daughter, and probably also during the forty years that Moses resided in Midian after he fled Egypt. But once they were reunited, these three siblings led God's people in the exodus and journeyed across the wilderness together as a family. The celebration that is recorded in Exodus 15 was precipitated by the miraculous event in which God parted the Red Sea and allowed His people to go through on dry ground. Once they were across, and with the armies of Pharaoh in hot pursuit, Moses extended his hand over the water and it came crashing down over the Egyptians, killing all of them.

Exodus 14:30–31 records the deliverance and its impact on God's people: *So the LORD saved Israel that day out of the hand of the Egyptians, and Israel saw the Egyptians dead on the seashore. Thus Israel saw the great work which the LORD had done in Egypt; so the people feared the LORD, and believed the LORD and His servant Moses.* This miracle caused Moses and Miriam to write the first song recorded in Scripture, and Miriam is the first recorded female worship leader. Their song of deliverance can be found in Exodus 15:1–21.

For more than three hundred and fifty years, God's people had suffered oppression and persecution in Egypt. Against the dramatic backdrop of God's supernatural display of power, Moses erupted in a song of praise to God, and Miriam the prophetess reached down, picked up a timbrel—which is similar to a tambourine—and led the women in dancing and in singing choruses at intervals throughout the song. They rejoiced with the words, *I will sing to the LORD, for He has triumphed gloriously!* (verse 1) Here we have a picture of God's people being 100 percent occupied with God. They had a reason to sing because this wasn't an escape on their part, it was a deliverance! There is a distinct difference between the words *escape* and *deliverance*. In an escape, the person assumes the active role. In a deliverance, God assumes the active role; everyone else is simply following along.

One Sunday morning as my husband and I were getting ready for church, our son left for Elsinore, California, where he was going to lead worship at a church that morning. It was raining, not heavily, but just enough to soak everything down. It hadn't rained for a while, so when the first drops fell, the oil rose to the surface of the highway and it became slippery. My son was in the right hand lane, keeping up with the traffic flow, when he hit a patch of water. His truck hydroplaned across all four lanes of the freeway into the fast lane where he did a double 360-degree turn before skidding off the road into the dirt and hitting the guardrail. He missed all the oncoming traffic and his truck got no more than a scratch on it. That was the moment he called home. As parents, we don't like getting those calls, but I knew when I heard the story that it wasn't an escape, but a miraculous deliverance on the part of God! For the remainder of the day, every time I thought about what had happened, I praised the Lord since there was nothing my son could have done to get out of that situation. It was God's protection. I told him he wore out another angel that day; he's worn out several more since then!

Psalm 34:1–3 says, *I will bless the LORD at all times; His praise shall continually be in my mouth. My soul shall make its boast in the LORD; the humble shall hear of it and be glad. Oh, magnify the LORD with me, and let us exalt His name together.* That's how it should be. When was the last time you paused and praised God for your deliverance out of darkness and into the kingdom of light, or for your deliverance from a trial? We forget to thank Him. Psalm 107:1–2 says, *Oh, give thanks to the LORD, for He is good! For His mercy endures forever. Let the redeemed of the LORD say so.* We should praise Him spontaneously, wholeheartedly, and simply for who He is. He deserves it. He is worthy of it.

In scene three, Miriam's pride is highlighted, along with the penalty she endured as a result. Numbers 12:1–15 records her downfall: *Then Miriam and Aaron spoke against Moses because of the Ethiopian woman whom he had married. . . . So they said, "Has the LORD indeed spoken only through Moses? Has He not spoken through us also?" And the LORD heard it. (Now the man Moses was very humble, more than all men who were on the face of the earth.) Suddenly the LORD said to Moses, Aaron, and Miriam, "Come out, you three, to the tabernacle of meeting!" So the three came out. Then the LORD came down in the pillar of cloud and stood in the door of the tabernacle, and called Aaron and Miriam. And they both went forward. Then He said, "Hear now My words: If there is a prophet among you, I, the LORD, make Myself known to him in a vision; I speak to him in a dream. Not so with My servant Moses; he is faithful in all My house. I speak with him face to face, even plainly, and not in dark sayings; and he sees the form of the LORD. Why then were you not afraid to speak against My servant Moses?"*

So the anger of the LORD was aroused against them, and He departed. And when the cloud departed from above the tabernacle, suddenly Miriam became leprous, as white as snow. Then Aaron turned toward Miriam, and there she was, a leper. So Aaron said to Moses, "Oh, my lord! Please do not lay this sin on us, in which we have done foolishly and in which we have sinned. Please do not let her be as one dead, whose flesh is half consumed when he comes out of his mother's womb!" So Moses cried out to the LORD, saying, "Please heal her, O God, I pray!" Then the LORD said to Moses, "If her father had but spit in her face, would she not be shamed seven days? Let her be shut out of the camp seven days, and after that she may be received again." So Miriam was shut out of the camp seven days, and the people did not journey on till Miriam was brought in again.

What a remarkable story. More than eighty years had passed since Miriam stood near the river to watch and see what would become of her baby brother. By all accounts, she had grown up to become a prophetess, a gifted musician, and a leader of the Hebrew women. She was probably invited to sit at the counsel table with her brothers since she occupied a position of honor among her people.

At some point during the journey across the desert, Miriam became concerned about the wife of Moses. We don't know whether the Ethiopian woman mentioned here was Zipporah, the wife he took when he resided in Midian, or whether she had died, and he had taken a second wife. Whoever she was, her presence was the cause for apprehension and criticism from Miriam and Aaron. They were not concerned about her race or skin color; they were concerned that she was a foreigner. On the surface, this seems justifiable because

God's people were commanded not to intermarry with foreigners. Those that intermarried usually ended up leaving God when their spouses turned their hearts to idol worship. So it seems that it was a viable concern, but one that was not justified in regard to Moses.

The second complaint was aimed directly at Moses and his leadership. At the core of their grievance was jealousy of their brother's number one position as leader over Israel. The three siblings had led the nation across the wilderness together, but due to a change in the leadership structure recorded in chapter 11, Miriam and Aaron decided that they were being slighted. Seventy new elders had been appointed in Israel. They were not only sharing the burden of responsibility, but also sharing the same anointing from the Holy Spirit that God had placed upon Moses, and they were prophesying. While Moses saw the addition of these elders as a much-needed asset, Miriam apparently viewed it as a threat to her position. Verse 1 says that *Miriam and Aaron spoke against Moses*. The Hebrew verb that is used here is the feminine/singular, meaning that Miriam was the real instigator in this situation. Aaron probably agreed with the initial concern over Moses' wife, but he may not have been motivated by jealousy as his sister was. She is mentioned first and was the only one struck with leprosy as a consequence.

Proverbs 16:18 says, *Pride goes before destruction, and a haughty spirit before a fall*. Even someone as godly as Miriam was not above being tempted by this sin, and perhaps the saddest part of Miriam's failure is that it was a very public one. It's bad enough when pride gets hold of a leader, but it is worse when that leader vents her disagreement with others in public, because it sows discord among the brethren. Proverbs 6 lists seven deadly sins that God hates, and sowing discord among the brethren is included in that list.

Hebrews 12:15 warns, *See to it that no one comes short of the grace of God; that no root of bitterness springing up causes trouble, and by it many be defiled* (NASB). That is exactly what happened to Miriam. Unless bitterness is dealt with before it takes root in a heart, it will spring up and cause trouble, defiling many others. Miriam allowed jealousy to become bitterness, which led to public criticism and embarrassment for her brother. She also allowed her own bitterness to defile her other brother, Aaron. And then she used her position to undermine Moses' authority, causing the people to question and doubt his leadership. The Lord heard it, and verse 4 says that He spoke *suddenly*. The Hebrew root word here means "in a wink" or "instantly." God acted swiftly in dealing with this sin. He called all three leaders to the tent of meeting, and there He singled out Miriam and Aaron to stand before Him. He told them that His relationship with Moses was different than His relationship with them or with any other prophet because He spoke with Moses face to face. Based on that fact alone, God demanded to know why they weren't afraid to speak out against His servant.

God says in His Word that He shows Himself holy to those who are near Him. When we read His Word, we are near Him and He reveals His holiness to us. He puts His finger on areas in our lives that aren't pleasing to Him, like when we let jealousy take root, and allow it to become bitterness, defiling those around us.

Verse 9 says, *The anger of the LORD burned against them and He departed* (NASB). God's anger burned not just against Miriam, but against Aaron too. However, because her role was greater, so were the consequences, and she was struck with leprosy. We read that lightly, but leprosy was a horrible condition. It was a highly infectious, communicable disease that would manifest itself in different stages of development. Miriam's leprosy appeared instantly, and it appeared at the peak of the disease's ravaging effects, giving her skin a totally white appearance. Because leprosy was so contagious, those who contracted it were required to separate themselves from everyone else. Any time someone approached the infected person, they were required by law to cry out, *Unclean! Unclean!* Can you imagine how Miriam felt? What a shameful position she had created for herself.

In the end, Miriam's leprosy was healed, but she spent seven days outside the camp. During that time, the whole nation of Israel was forced to wait for her return before they could move forward. That meant the entire nation knew what she had done, what the result was, and the shame she had to bear. Isn't it humiliating enough when we know what we have done? Or when our family or closest friends know? Imagine if you saw your face and heard your voice on the six o'clock news, meaning that thousands upon thousands of people knew of your sin. If that's not bad enough, what if everyone else's lives were put on hold until you dealt with the consequences of your wrongdoing? We need to realize that our choices affect the lives of those around us, sometimes in a very big way.

Miriam was healed at the end of those seven days as instantly as she had received the disease, but not before Moses had prayed on her behalf. The brother who was the object of her scorn, derision, and criticism pleaded with God to heal her. But God wasn't willing to restore her immediately. She had to deal with the consequences first because her rebellion was not only against Moses; the bottom line was that she rebelled against God. We have to get to the place in our Christian lives where we recognize that our rebellion is not against others alone. There is a much deeper root, and sometimes God will force us to face the consequences so that we will recognize and deal with the fact that we are rebelling against Him.

During those seven days, Miriam must have come to the point of repentance because God restored her to fellowship in the congregation. She must have had a huge heart change as she looked back and thought about those early years—her love for God, her walk with Him, and how much that relationship meant. God restored Miriam because His judgment goes hand-in-hand with His forgiveness.

What happened to Miriam—this one who had such keen discernment and intellect when she was so young; this one who faithfully cared for her brothers, showing them such compassion; this one who dedicated her life to serving her God and her nation? What caused her to get off course when she was in her nineties? We don't know exactly where she went wrong, but her life stands as an example of lessons in stark contrast. It teaches us both what to do and what not to do. She started out so well, but ended with such disappointment. Any one of us could just as easily fall into the same trap as Miriam if we take our eyes off the Lord.

Has God called you to lead the women in your church or to speak on His behalf? Has He called you to be a worship leader? Has He put a desire in your heart to be a leader among women? If you are in a leadership position or you have a desire to be, I want you to consider the following questions: Are you more concerned with having your own way than with being a team player? Do you care more about how other people see you than how God sees you? Are you perhaps struggling with someone who is in a position of authority over you? Have you spoken out against that individual in public? Are you feeling neglected by those around you in the ministry? Do you find yourself nursing petty grievances rather than dealing with them? If you answered yes to any of the above questions, then you are potentially in danger of falling into the same sin as Miriam.

Tuck the following three Scripture references away for those times when you need a heart check-up. The first is Jeremiah 45:5: *Are you seeking great things for yourself? Do not seek them* (NASB). Jeremiah's warning here is not against ambition because that is not bad in itself. What he means is, *Are you seeking from a self-centered ambition in order to gain things for yourself?* Someone has said about serving others, *A true leader will put back into life more than she takes out of it.* Miriam did that, and we should do that as well. The question you and I must repeatedly ask ourselves is: *What is my heart motive?* That's what God cares about.

The second verse is Proverbs 4:23, which tells us, *Keep your heart with all diligence, for out of it spring the issues of life.* The word *keep* here means "to guard carefully." This is our responsibility, not God's. If we allow jealousy to remain unchecked in the heart, it will eventually manifest itself in criticism from the mouth every time, guaranteed! Jesus told His followers, *Out of the abundance of the heart the mouth speaks* (Matthew 12:34). If we nurse petty grievances and don't deal with them, eventually they will come spilling out, causing a whole lot of trouble, not only for us, but also for the people around us, resulting in many being robbed of true joy and fulfillment.

The last verse I want you to file away is Romans 13:1: *Every person is to be in subjection to the governing authorities. For there is no authority except from God, and those which exist are established by God* (NASB). If we are to understand what this verse says, then we must understand that any struggle with authority is a struggle with God Himself. The prophet Daniel stated that *He* [God] *removes kings and establishes kings* (2:21, NASB). This does not mean that everyone in authority will always do the will of God, but it does mean that if we willingly submit to authority, God will use our submission for good in our lives.

Miriam fell because she thought she could do a better job. The problem with her thinking was that God did not place her in the lead role. Moses only needed one thing to qualify for the position—the call of God. His call is the only thing that you and I will ever need. This gifted, incredible woman of God left a caution for every leader to heed: God alone chooses and places people in positions of leadership. He raises up and puts down, and He does not want to be questioned or challenged on His choices. In the end, Miriam served God and her people well into her nineties, and as a result, five books in Scripture—Exodus, Numbers, Deuteronomy, Chronicles, and Micah—record something about her.

As you look into the spectrum of Miriam's life, perhaps you see a few resemblances to your own. If you learn from her failures as well as her successes, then her legacy will have a lasting impact, making you a better person.

A man named James R. Sizoo said, *Let it never be forgotten that glamour is not greatness; applause is not fame; prominence is not eminence. The man [or woman] of the hour is not apt to be the man [or woman] of the ages. A stone may sparkle, but that does not make it a diamond; people may have money, but that does not make them a success. It is what the unimportant people do that really counts and determines the course of history. The greatest forces in the universe are never spectacular. Summer showers are more effective than hurricanes, but they get no publicity. The world would soon die but for the fidelity, loyalty, and consecration of those whose names are unhonored and unsung.*[1] May our goal in life be to wholeheartedly follow and please the One who created us for His own pleasure and glory. If we make it our aim to be well-pleasing to Him, He will take care of our legacy to the world.

Reflections

1. Take a moment and review the three scenes from Miriam's life.
2. Throughout her life, she exhibited a variety of positive and negative characteristics. Which do you identify with most and why?
3. How can you avoid her mistakes and guard your heart motives?
4. Miriam left a lasting legacy of both successes and failures. What kind of legacy are you leaving? Be specific.
5. Ask the Lord to enable you to leave a heritage of fidelity, loyalty, and consecration.

---

[1] Sizoo, James R. "Bits & Pieces." Posted November 8, 2000. *WIT and WISDOM*™ *E-zine*. www.witandwisdom.org. (Accessed July 15, 2004.)

About the Author

Jan Vance's greatest joy in life is that she and Dennis, her husband of thirty-six years, and their twenty-eight-year old son, David, are all serving the Lord! Her greatest passion is seeing Christian women discover who they are in Christ and where they fit into His body.

Jan has been a part of Harvest Christian Fellowship in Riverside, California, for the past twenty-six years. She credits a good deal of her growth as a Christian to following after mature, godly women in the Calvary Chapel movement whose lives greatly impacted hers. She has served as the director of Harvest Women's Ministries for the past fifteen years. In addition to overseeing the events at one of the ten largest churches in the nation, she has been a teacher with Women's Bible Fellowship for twenty years and has written curriculum for the study for the past twelve years. Jan has co-authored over twenty lesson series from the Old and New Testaments, including lessons on twenty-one women of the Bible. Those lessons are currently being used at churches throughout the United States.

Jan believes her call at this season of life is to write, teach, and help disciple leaders in women's ministry. Her favorite pastimes include reading, walking, thinking, and spending time investing in the lives of women who are in passionate pursuit of God's will for their lives.

He wants to do a wonder in us. It isn't what we do, how we clean up our lives, or the rules that we follow. All He needs is a willing vessel, a woman who will simply say, I yield my life to You...

—Gail Mays

Esther

A Woman of Purpose

by Gail Mays

For if thou altogether holdest thy peace at this time, then shall there enlargement and deliverance arise to the Jews from another place; but thou and thy father's house shall be destroyed: and who knoweth whether thou art come to the kingdom for such a time as this?
Then Esther bade them return Mordecai this answer,
Go, gather together all the Jews that are present in Shushan, and fast ye for me, and neither eat nor drink three days, night or day: I also and my maidens will fast likewise; and so will I go in unto the king, which is not according to the law: and if I perish, I perish.
—Esther 4:14–16, KJV

I was saved during the Jesus Movement, the great revival that swept through our nation and then throughout the world in the late 1960s and early 1970s. Jesus touched me one day, I gave my life to Him, and I've never regretted it. The passion that burned in me the first day I came to know the Lord as a lost hippie continues to grow more than thirty years later.

Esther was a woman who had a great passion for the Lord. Corrie ten Boom once said, *God has plans—not problems—for our lives.*[1]

---

[1] ten Boom, Corrie . "The Joy-Filled Life." *In Touch Ministries. www.intouch.org.* (Accessed August 5, 2004.)

This is an important concept. Through her experiences in the concentration camps and the Holocaust, Corrie discovered that God knows no problems, only plans. Esther was faced with what seemed like an insurmountable problem, yet God had a great plan.

By way of introduction to Esther, I would like to welcome you to queen school because when God gets hold of a woman, she becomes a queen. The story of Esther is one in which the Lord took a *nobody* and made her a *somebody*. The heart of Esther's story is found in Esther 4:14–16. Esther's uncle, Mordecai, pleaded with her to go before the king on behalf of her people, the Jews, who were about to be annihilated. Esther's famous declaration in response to her uncle's request, *If I perish, I perish* (verse 16), is not a declaration of fear, hopelessness, or resignation. Rather, Esther was making a vow before the Lord that speaks of many different things. First, it speaks of Esther's relationship with God. By making this declaration, she was actually saying that she was surrendering her life to God and committing herself to be His *doulos*, or bondslave. She was saying, *I'm at Your disposal, Lord.* We are not our own. The Lord Jesus owns us, and the life He has planned for us will be the best life we could possibly live. Therefore, we are wise to surrender everything to Him. Esther's relationship with God was such that she could say, *Do whatever You want with me.*

Second, Esther's words speak of her confidence in God. She was testifying of her assurance that God would not give her more than she could handle without providing a way of escape. Third, her vow speaks of her tremendous faith in God. She did not limit the unlimited God. She was declaring that she believed in miracles and in a God who specializes in impossible situations. Do you have one of those hanging around your life anywhere? They are the Lord's specialty. If we had the answers for every situation, why would we need the Lord? And so, the phrase, *If I perish, I perish*, is a loaded phrase.

The name of God is never mentioned in the book of Esther, yet His hand is visible from beginning to end. Divine providence was at work in Esther's life. Believing in God's divine providence means recognizing the hand of God in all that comes our way. Maybe we don't understand it, but we know God is at work. Trusting in God's divine plan means remembering that His presence is with us—even though we can't explain or even comprehend it. The Spirit of God imparts the knowledge to us that the Lord is with us, in us, and around us. He leads and guides, pushes and prods, encourages and comforts, and convinces and convicts us to do certain things. He also gives us the assurance that He will protect us, provide for our every need, reward us, and do the impossible.

The theme throughout the book of Esther is that God moves people and governments in order to accomplish His will. The affairs of the United States and the world are not in the hands of government officials, but in God's hands. When we look at a world that is uncertain and full of violence and hatred, recognizing the providence of God gives us the confidence that He is at work getting the world ready for Jesus' second coming.

God orchestrates events to accomplish His plan for us as well. He moves people into our lives to test us—like sandpaper wearing down some of our rough edges. Sometimes He removes people, and there's a great void, or He moves us from one city or state to another in order to accomplish His will. When we are aware that the hand of God is in all that comes our way, we will see that our lives are full of miracles and divine intervention.

The book of Esther is a thrilling story about romance, feasts, fasts, power, banquets, pride, deception, courage, challenge, sacrifice, and celebration. It begins with beauty treatments and a beauty contest, then it escalates into a major crisis, but in the end

God turns the tables. What the enemy meant as a device for the destruction of God's people became the very thing used to destroy that same enemy. It's an awesome book that reminds us that God will always be the winner. Never forget that as daughters of God, we are on the winning side!

This story begins not with Queen Esther, but with Queen Vashti, who was removed from her position for disobeying the king. She was banished from the kingdom, and the search for a new queen began. Esther, a forgotten orphan in the massive Persian empire, was one of many beauties brought to the palace for the competition to replace Vashti. She pleased the king, and was chosen to become queen. Meanwhile, Mordecai, Esther's uncle and adoptive father, became a government official and refused to bow to the wicked prime minister, Haman. It bothered Haman to no end that this man would not bow to him because everyone else in the kingdom showed him reverence. Because Mordecai refused to bow to anyone but God, Haman was determined to kill him. But he was not satisfied to simply kill Mordecai. He wanted to destroy the entire Jewish race, and had a decree written directing that all Jews be massacred on a certain day. (There were about three million Jews living in the Persian empire at the time.)

Esther was challenged to step in and save her people. She didn't have to get involved. It was within her own free will to decide whether or not she would be a part of the great work God wanted to accomplish through her. She chose to say yes to God, and became His woman of the hour.

I see a few things when I look at this story. I see the possibilities; I see the plot; I see the plan; I see the passion; and, as she touches the golden scepter, I see power released. God was able to pour His Spirit through a woman who simply made herself available, and an entire nation was saved.

The principle of *possibility* is the first thing I would like us to think about. The remoteness of the chance that Esther would ever become queen is absolutely staggering. She had to be the most unlikely candidate. She was an unknown orphan, she was not of the right race, and she didn't have the right clothes. Representatives of the king went throughout this massive empire looking for the most beautiful women to compete in a beauty contest at which the king would select the queen of his choice. The empire was made up of one hundred twenty-seven provinces. That doesn't mean there were only one hundred twenty-seven women in this beauty contest; it could have included thousands of women. Esther had no experience that would have prepared her to become a queen. She didn't have royal blood and she had not gone to *queen school*. In fact, she had nothing going for her except that God looked at her and saw possibilities, just as He does with us.

You and I look at ourselves and think, *What do I have to offer? How could God use me?* Or we reflect on our backgrounds, perhaps our lack of education, and think, *I've made such a mess of things.* Or we wonder if we will ever rise above our failures and walk in victory. A few of us could say, *If they had a contest for the most dysfunctional family, I think I could win.* Some of these issues are excuses while others are serious concerns about whether or not we would qualify to be a servant in God's kingdom. God looks at us and He sees possibilities. He wants to do a wonder in us. It isn't what we do, how we clean up our lives, or the rules that we follow. All He needs is a willing vessel, a woman who will simply say, *I yield my life to You—I yield all that I am, and all that I'm not. I yield my strengths along with my weaknesses. I yield my joys, my sorrows, my pain, my hopes, my hopelessness, my dreams, and my shattered dreams.* We lay it all at His feet and offer ourselves to Him: *Here I am, Lord. I'm at Your disposal. Do a work in me that will make the world stand in awe and say, "There is no way that that could be her. I know her too well. This has to be a work of the Lord."* The possibilities are endless.

Second, I want us to think about the *plan* of God in this story. Esther was born at a particular moment in history. We do not decide the time or place of our birth, or our nationality. Esther was born *for such a time as this.* God brought her to the kingdom to do a work, just as He brings each of us to the kingdom to do a work. He created us and ordained our birth. He put us in a particular family, in a certain area, and made us a certain race. He has brought us to the kingdom *for such a time as this* (Esther 4:14). The question is, *what will your vow be?* Will you accept what the Lord would have you to do? Will you trust in Him enough to say with Esther, *If I perish, I perish?*

Esther was brought before the king, and in the midst of all these beautiful women, he looked at her and said, *My search is over. This is my woman!* He crowned her queen and all was wonderful. Esther was enjoying life. Maybe today you don't have any serious problems. Life is pretty good and blessings are pouring out upon you. Sometimes life is like that. Esther was living in the palace, hanging out with the girls. Can you imagine the talks and tea parties they must have had? The beauty treatments, the clothes, and the shopping! She had a wealth of queenly privileges.

Then came trouble. Isn't that always the way it happens? A problem arises and 99 percent of the time, the problem is in the form of a person. Do you have a Haman in your life? Esther was oblivious to what was going on in the kingdom until Mordecai informed her: *Hey, listen. A plot has been set against us. That wicked Haman is going to destroy our people, and Esther, you've got to do something!* He challenged her to go before the king, even though it was against the law to do so without being summoned, and it had been more than thirty days since she had been called. The offense was punishable by death, but Mordecai encouraged her, saying, *Esther, think about it. Maybe you were made queen for this very moment. Perhaps God has brought you to the kingdom in order to work through you to save a nation. Be not afraid. Be courageous. God is with you.*

We have to realize that we have an Enemy in this life. We cannot be oblivious to the way he works. But never forget that God has a plan. Though you and I have no clue as to why God allows certain things to happen in our lives, we can be sure He is strategically placing us in a certain place to accomplish His purpose. He has a work to do in and through each of us.

In verse 14, Mordecai said, *For if thou altogether holdeth thy peace at this time, then shall there enlargement and deliverance arise to the Jews from another place; but thou and thy father's house shall be destroyed: and who knoweth whether thou art come to the kingdom for such a time as this?* (KJV) God will not be without people to work in the kingdom. We don't have to comply and be a part of His plan if we don't want to. He wants to use willing vessels. Mordecai was warning Esther that if she held her peace, she would miss out on the greatest blessing that she could ever imagine. Serving the Lord is the greatest blessing of all.

Esther's fear was legitimate because Queen Vashti had been removed from the kingdom for a crime far less serious than appearing before the king without being summoned. This was a dreaded difficulty. Yet God knew it would arise. Are you facing a dreaded difficulty today? Are there things in your life that are unsettled? Perhaps you've even asked the question, *God, if You love me, why is this happening? I thought I was serving You and doing my best, and all of a sudden these bad things are happening. Don't You love me anymore, Lord? What have I done to deserve this?* God knew that your crisis would arise, and He has a plan. Trust Him even if you are afraid.

Third, I want to consider the *power* that was released. Verse 15 says, *Then Esther bade them return Mordecai this answer, Go, gather together all the Jews that are present in Shushan, and fast ye for me, and neither eat nor drink three days, night or day: I also and my maidens will fast likewise; and so will I go in unto the king, which is not according to the law: and if I perish, I perish* (KJV). The type of fast that Esther was calling for was not a weight loss fast or a medical fast. This fast was combined with prayer and implemented specifically to seek the plan of God. *What do You have in mind, Lord? What are You trying to tell us?* It was done in order to obtain wisdom, and to receive strength and protection for the impossible situation they were facing.

Esther believed in the power of prayer. Do you? The power of prayer is the most awesome force in the universe, and the prayer of the righteous avails much (James 5:16). Prayer moves the hand of God that moves man. In those impossible situations, when you're trying to find solutions and nothing is working—or when you might even be making matters worse, hit your knees. God said, *If my people, which are called by my name, shall humble themselves, and pray, and seek my face, and turn from their wicked ways, then will I hear from heaven, and will forgive their sin, and will heal their land* (2 Chronicles 7:14, KJV). Let these words be ignited within your heart as you think about the situations you are facing and as you look at how our nation has gone awry. If we will humble ourselves and pray, God will do great things.

The combination of prayer and fasting is the most powerful tool that God has entrusted to us as His children, especially when dealing with those dreaded difficulties in which our greatest fears are realized. For example, it is a wise approach when dealing with an unreasonable person. In conflicts that are impossible to resolve by human efforts, we are to pray and seek the mind of God. Jesus said some battles must be won through prayer and fasting, and it is amazing what God will do when we utilize these tools.

Esther's vow was, *If I perish, I perish*. If she didn't act, she and her entire race could be wiped out. God had brought her to this place and if her time was up, she knew that He would bring deliverance from some other source. She had come to the point of being willing to give her very life to follow Him. That is really what surrender requires. Surrender is a theological word that sometimes makes us shudder. The *old woman* within us doesn't want to surrender, but to the *new woman* in Christ, surrender is like a breath of fresh air.

He wants you to yield because you can't fix your situation anyway. Give it to Him. That's all He wants. He wants you to come to the point of not wanting to carry your burden and of being able to say, *If I perish, I perish*. There was a fire that burned inside of Esther, and God gave her courage and faith, along with deep insight, wisdom, and a love for His people. He will do the same for you when you surrender your life completely to Him.

Finally, I want us to think about the *passion* in this story. When Esther went before the king, she had to be dressed in her royal apparel in order to be accepted. She went into his throne room with fear and trembling, not knowing whether he was going to take her head off or accept her. But she found favor in his sight. He put forth the golden scepter, and Esther drew near and touched it. At that moment, wonder-working power was released and the king said, *What is your request, Queen Esther? You can have up to half my kingdom* (see Esther 5:3).

When passion begins to burn within us, God gives extraordinary power. We don't have the answers for the problems in our lives, but we can't just walk into the throne room and ask God to help us. We have to wear the right apparel by being cleansed in the blood of the Lamb and being born again. Then the privileges come. Any sinner is welcome. God doesn't turn anybody away. As we repent before Him, and are washed in His blood, we are able to draw near. He holds out the golden scepter. We touch it, and He asks, *What is your request?*

Passion burns within our lives for answers, for direction, for a decision, for help, for God's peace and strength, or for victory over the sins we are battling. With that passion, we are pressed to reach out to God. We want a touch from Him. The only way we're going to survive is to receive a touch from the Lord. When He reaches out His hand, we receive *dunamis* power, the power to live the Christian life, the power to die to self, and the power to walk in victory, love, and forgiveness. He then begins to pour His Spirit through us, and we become the woman of the hour in our day; we become the woman of influence who touches others for the Lord.

That was Esther's story and her time to see the hand of God arranging people and circumstances to accomplish His will, to see incredible things happen against all odds, to see the enemy defeated, God's people saved, and the land filled with gladness. But this is our time. This is our era in which God has brought us to the kingdom *for such a time as this.* It's our time to be women of influence, to be endued with power from on high, to sit at the feet of Jesus to get direction, and to be filled for service. Now is the time to have a passion for Jesus in order for God to unleash His power through us. In so doing, He'll give us all that we need to be a part of His unfolding plan.

Reflections

1. Stop and ponder Esther's rise from her position as a *nobody* to a *somebody.*

2. Despite all odds she was chosen as queen because God had a plan and a purpose. How does this encourage you to seek God's plan and purpose for your own life?

3. Do you have a Haman in your life? How are you responding to this difficulty?

4. Prayer and fasting are powerful weapons for defeating the Enemy. What steps can you take to incorporate them into your life? Be specific.

5. Take a moment to renew your passion for Him and ask Him to release His power in your life.

About the Author

Gail Mays is the wife of Senior Pastor Steve Mays, who has served at Calvary Chapel South Bay, located in the Los Angeles, California, area for twenty-five years. Gail and Steve have been a vital part of the Calvary Chapel movement for thirty-five years.

They were saved at the height of the revival known as the Jesus Movement. It's hard to believe, looking at Gail now, that she was once a flower child who sold and took drugs. Her life is a powerful testimony of how God can transform a ruined life into something that can be used for His glory and honor. She calls her testimony *But God* and recounts how she was repeatedly going one way BUT GOD intervened and wonderfully rescued her!

Gail has three grown children and five grandchildren. Though she is involved in a variety of activities, the one thing she loves to do most is minister to women. She takes every opportunity to instruct them in the Word of God, believing that it alone has the power to change a life!

As the sufferings come in, so does the comfort. The God of all comfort is the only One that can comfort us the way we need to be comforted.

—Karin Kyle

The Women with an Issue of Blood

A Woman in Need

by Karin Kyle

*Now a certain woman had a flow of blood for twelve years, and had
suffered many things from many physicians. She had spent all that she
had and was no better, but rather grew worse. When she heard about
Jesus, she came behind Him in the crowd and touched His garment;
for she said, "If only I may touch His clothes, I shall be made well."
Immediately the fountain of her blood was dried up, and she felt in
her body that she was healed of the affliction. And Jesus, immediately
knowing in Himself that power had gone out of Him, turned around
in the crowd and said, "Who touched My clothes?"
But His disciples said to Him, "You see the multitude thronging
You, and You say, 'Who touched Me?'" And He looked around to
see her who had done this thing. But the woman, fearing and
trembling, knowing what had happened to her, came and fell down
before Him and told Him the whole truth. And He said to her,
"Daughter, your faith has made you well. Go in peace, and be
healed of your affliction."*
—Mark 5:25–34

Imagine being in the midst of your family and community, but
never being allowed to touch another person or even sit on the couch

and talk with them. The woman who touched the hem of Jesus' garment lived an isolated life for so long that she became desperate enough to violate a host of cultural taboos in pursuit of healing.

In Leviticus chapter 15 we learn that according to ceremonial law, a menstruating woman was considered unclean for the seven days or so that she was bleeding. This nameless woman, who is commonly referred to as *The Woman and the Issue of Blood*, had a flow of blood that did not stop for twelve full years, which means she was considered unclean for more than a decade. Being unclean meant that whatever she touched, whether an object or another person, would then also be considered unclean.

Think about the life she must have led. We don't know if she was married or single, or whether or not she had children. If she was married, her condition would have produced such heartache. And if she had children, they would never have been permitted to reach their arms up for a hug from their mom, or they too would have been made unclean. God created us with the need to be loved physically, but for this woman human touch was impossible.

Her condition probably included not only the blood flow and uncleanness, but also discomfort or pain. She was suffering with a terrible affliction. All the expectations and hope that she had placed in man to find a cure had failed. Verse 26 says that she had spent all her money and suffered many things from a multitude of physicians, but only became worse. She desperately went from one physician to another just as we often try different remedies and doctors. When you are afflicted with either a life threatening or painful condition, you may become desperate. You want to feel better and are willing to do whatever it takes, no matter the cost. When my grandpa had cancer, he tried absolutely everything to cure it. He even went to Mexico for treatments, but it didn't do any good. He died before I was a Christian, but I have great hope that he is in heaven because my mom remembers seeing a Billy Graham book by his bedside as his life drew to a close.

Man had let this woman down. She grew more and more ill until her hopes and expectations were shattered, and there was nothing left to do. But then, according to verse 27, she heard about Jesus, a very popular healer who was preaching and teaching all over Galilee. This news would get your hopes up: *Maybe if I go to this man He can heal me!* With renewed anticipation, she went to find Him. Perhaps she was thinking, *I don't need to talk to Him or embrace Him; if I could just touch that hem, maybe I will be healed.*

When she saw Jesus, she stopped at nothing to reach Him. Verse 24 says the crowds were pressing into Him. His twelve disciples and Jairus, the ruler of the synagogue, were with Him because Jesus was on His way to heal this man's daughter. Picture Jesus in the middle of this large crowd with everybody touching Him and wanting something from Him. If you are my age or a little older, you might remember images of those crazy girls trying to touch one of the Beatles. I'm not knowledgeable about today's popular music scene, but I'm sure that still goes on. People want to touch their hero, and this woman wanted to get to Jesus. However, she would have made everyone and everything she brushed up against ceremonially unclean as she tried to reach Jesus, including Him. She had her eyes fixed upon Him and as soon as she touched the hem of His robe, she immediately felt the blood flow stop and knew that she was healed.

Can you imagine the joy that would have overwhelmed her after twelve years of suffering with that affliction? Most of us face some sort of infirmity, perhaps a little thing that comes and goes, or maybe something that lingers. It feels so wonderful when it's gone, though! What a thrill it must have been, after twelve years of both physical infirmity and emotional pain, to realize, *I'm healed. I can hug someone. I can have a relationship with someone.*

Jesus knew something supernatural had happened. He turned around and asked, *Who touched My clothes?* (verse 30) The disciples must have been incredulous when He asked that question. They must have echoed, *Who touched You? Right, everybody's touching You. What do You mean, who touched You?* (see verse 31) Luke 8:46 tells us that Jesus said, *Somebody touched Me, for I perceived power going out from Me.* Other people were pressing in on Him, but this woman, because of her desperation and her faith, touched Him and was healed.

Jesus looked through the crowd. The woman was still close by and she heard what He said. What was she thinking? *Okay, now He knows, I didn't think He would know. I only wanted to be healed.* He saw her, and of course, He knew she was the one who had done it. I wonder what His face looked like at that moment. The Bible says His eyes are like a refining fire, but within them are compassion and grace. When He made eye contact with her, I envision compassion written all over His face because she responded in humility, bowing before Him and confessing everything. As she spoke, the crowd heard what had happened: *I thought to myself, "If I only could get to Him," and then I did, and this is what happened. And how wonderful!* (see verse 33) Jesus could have healed her and continued on without comment, but He wanted personal contact with her. He wanted her to know: *I am not just a healer, I'm a Savior, I'm your Lord, and I'm your friend.*

Think about the extent of this woman's faith. She had enough to conclude, *Here is a man who is healing people and I want to be healed.* She didn't know anything beyond that. But when she reached out and touched the hem of His garment, He responded by honoring that small act, and said, *Your faith has made you well. Go in peace, and be healed of your affliction* (verse 34).

We all suffer in different ways and at different times of our lives. Whether it is physical, relational, financial, or something else, everyone goes through affliction. Second Corinthians 4:16 says, *We do not lose heart. Even though our outward man is perishing . . .* If you have a health problem like this woman had, your outward man is perishing, but Paul goes on to say that your *inward man is being renewed day by day. For our light affliction, which is but for a moment, is working for us a far more exceeding and eternal weight of glory, while we do not look at the things which are seen, but at the things which are not seen. For the things which are seen are temporary, but the things which are not seen are eternal* (verses 16–18). God has a plan and a purpose for everything. These trials are working *for* us, not against us. Elisabeth Elliot's book, *A Path Through Suffering,* is a wonderful resource for regaining perspective and learning to take your eyes off yourself and your problems, and focusing instead on the Lord and His purposes.

We suffer for many reasons. Second Corinthians 1:3–4 says our God is *the Father of mercies and God of all comfort, who comforts us in all our tribulation,* that we may be able to comfort others. If we haven't received comfort because we haven't suffered, how could we pass it on? We suffer for the world's sake and also for Christ's sake so that He will be revealed in us. He works everything together for good to conform us into the image of His Son (Romans 8:28–29). He uses different circumstances to make us into what He wants us to be. He may work in my life in an entirely different way than He will in your life. We look at other people's trials and think, *I could not endure that,* but that is because we're not in it and He hasn't given us grace for it. We only have grace for the moment. We can't plan it ahead of time. We have to understand that if the Lord allows the trial, like this woman's twelve-year flow of blood, we'll be able to handle it because He will equip us and give us strength.

Many of us, especially before we knew the Lord, put all of our hopes and expectations in man. We searched everywhere for the answer to our afflictions. Some of us were suffering financially and tried every *get-rich* program out there. Others felt like a *nobody* and pursued a career that would guarantee prestige so we could make a name for ourselves. Still others sought fulfillment through relationships. Man does not have the answer. Doctors do not have the answer. The only way to go to a doctor is with the knowledge that God is with you, guiding them for your sake. Often the primary reason we came to know the Lord is because we put our hope and trust in man, and he let us down, leaving us worse off than before.

We can gain new hope like this woman who heard about Jesus and went to Him. Psalm 62:5 says, *My soul, wait silently for God alone, for my expectation is from Him.* He is the only hope we have. Our hope cannot be in a friend, a husband, a child, a job, a car, or a home. No one and nothing else can help us—Jesus is the only hope.

However, sometimes after we walk with the Lord for a while, it is easy to slip back into putting our hope and expectations in man's ways and answers. Is God still your first hope? Ask yourself: *When I am afflicted, whether financially, relationally, physically, or in whatever way, is He my first hope?* Or do you first put your trust in the medicine cabinet, the telephone, or the bank account? Are you as determined as this woman was to get to Jesus? Do you go to Him knowing that He is the solution? Do you spend time with Him, reaching out to grab the hem of His garment? This woman could have let fear stop her—fear of knowing she would make everyone unclean and fear of the ridicule that would inevitably follow. Or she could have worried, *What if He doesn't heal me?* These thoughts were probably going through her mind, but she was determined to get past them. Does fear stop you from reaching out to Jesus?

If not fear, does unbelief, complacency, or apathy stop you from going to the Lord? Proverbs 13:4 says, *The soul of the sluggard craves, and gets nothing* (NIV). A lot of us want to be healed, or relieved of an affliction, or restored relationally, but we do nothing and therefore we lack. We don't go to the Lord. We are not determined enough because it's too much work to pray.

If you have a physical affliction, do you obey James 5:14–15, which says, *Is anyone among you sick? Let him call for the elders of the church, and let them pray over him, anointing him with oil in the name of the Lord. And the prayer of faith will save the sick?* I wonder how many of us are afflicted, and yet don't ask for prayer. I was so blessed one Sunday night when my husband, Damian, invited the physically afflicted to come forward for prayer. What a wonderful, wonderful time for God's people. Where is your faith when it comes to obeying that Scripture? Maybe the Lord wants to use the elders of your church to heal you.

What kind of faith do you have? Do you have an active, living faith in the Lord? We sing that song, *I Know You Can Do All Things*, but do we believe the words? If you have doubt and fear, your prayer should be like the man who said, *Lord, I believe but help my unbelief,* because faith pleases the heart of God. Hebrews 11:6 says, *Without faith it is impossible to please Him, for he who comes to God must believe that He is, and that He is a rewarder of those who diligently seek Him.* Without faith it is impossible to please Him, so if you have faith, then you are going to please Him. You must trust the Lord, knowing that your heavenly Father can take care of your problems, and that Jesus blesses those who seek Him and believe.

Sometimes our prayers are answered in obvious accord with what we have prayed. At other times when we pray, He does not answer the way we want. First John 5:14–15 says, *If we ask anything according to His will, He hears us. And if we know that He hears us, whatever we ask, we know that we have the petitions that we have asked of Him.* So we have to pray, *Lord, I would like to be healed of this, yet not my will but Yours be done.* In 2 Corinthians 12:7–9, Paul describes his long-term physical ailment as a messenger from Satan. He says he sought the

Lord three times for the removal of this affliction, but God's answer was, *My grace is sufficient for you, for My strength is made perfect in weakness.* That was probably not the answer Paul wanted. Most likely, he would rather have been relieved of his suffering.

Throughout my walk with the Lord, I've said, *I don't get it, Lord. You are a big God; You could heal all these people who love You,* yet God is on the throne and He knows. I do not understand why He doesn't heal some people. It is beyond my comprehension and it breaks my heart, but I trust that the Lord has a plan and a purpose. Second Corinthians 1:5 promises, *For as the sufferings of Christ abound in us, so our consolation* [or comfort] *also abounds through Christ.* I love that. As the sufferings come in, so does the comfort. The God of all comfort is the only One that can comfort us the way we need to be comforted.

Whatever your affliction is today, the answer is to trust in Jesus, run to Jesus, and rest in Jesus. Maybe you're like the woman in this story and all you need to do is to reach out and touch the hem of His garment in order to be healed. Maybe you are like Paul and He will simply say to you, *My grace is sufficient, because My strength is made perfect in weakness and what I want to do through your life through this suffering is more glorious than any earthly healing.* He is working in you a far more exceeding and eternal weight of glory. In Romans 8:18, Paul says, *I reckon that the sufferings of this present time are not worthy to be compared with the glory which shall be revealed in us* (KJV).

Maybe your faith—whether it's faith to be healed or faith to endure—will speak words like those Jesus spoke to Jairus after this woman was healed. People said to Jairus, *Let the teacher go; your daughter is dead. Don't trouble Him* (see Mark 5:35). Can you imagine hearing those words: *Your daughter is dead?* Jesus immediately looked at him and said, *Do not be afraid; only believe* (verse 36). Let your faith inspire those around you and give them encouragement to trust and believe.

Reflections

1. Pause and reflect on the story of this woman's desperate situation.
2. What spiritual lessons do you discover in this story?
3. What overwhelming circumstances have you personally experienced (spiritual, emotional, physical, relational), and how did you respond to them?
4. How does Jesus' response to this woman encourage you to trust in His power to meet your need?
5. In what areas do you need a touch from the Lord? Take a moment to bring them before the Lord in prayer, trusting Him to meet your need, and giving praise for His unfailing love and compassion.

———

About the Author

Karin Kyle has been very happily married to Damian Kyle, senior pastor of Calvary Chapel Modesto, California, for twenty-eight years. She is the mother of two married daughters and grandmother to four grandchildren. Karin gave her life to the Lord in 1981 and moved to Modesto with her family in June 1985 to start Calvary Chapel Modesto. Karin oversees the women's ministry and has been teaching the ladies' Bible study for nineteen years. Her life verse is Luke 1:38, *Then Mary said, "Behold the maidservant of the Lord! Let it be to me according to your word...."* and her desire is to always and completely surrender to the Lord's will.

Nothing happens with God by chance.
It isn't by chance that we land in a
particular place at a particular time to
fulfill a particular need.

—June Hesterly

Ruth and Naomi

Women Redeemed

By June Hesterly

*Then they lifted up their voices and wept again; and Orpah
kissed her mother-in-law, but Ruth clung to her. And she said,
"Look, your sister-in-law has gone back to her people and to her
gods; return after your sister-in-law."
But Ruth said: "Entreat me not to leave you, or to turn back
from following after you; for wherever you go, I will go; and
wherever you lodge, I will lodge; your people shall be my people,
and your God, my God. Where you die, I will die, and there
will I be buried. The LORD do so to me, and more also, if anything but death parts you and me."*
—Ruth 1:14–17

A few years ago my grand-daughter, Amanda, who was about
five years old at the time, sent me a shoe box from her home in
Denver, Colorado. As I opened it, a few pebbles and beads rolled
out. Inside was a feather she had found, a dried and crumbling leaf
that she had admired, her school picture, and a self-portrait she had
drawn. Most precious of all was a bouquet of flowers she had picked
from her garden. In her child's mind she thought if she placed a wet
paper towel around the stem of the flowers they would still be fresh
when they reached her Grammy's house. However, when it arrived

in the mail, both the flowers and the paper towel were completely dry. What made this gift most precious was the shape of Amanda's hand that had dried into the paper towel. She had sent me her love in the shape of a handprint.

God's handprint is evident throughout the wonderful book of Ruth, showing us His providential care, His never-ending grace, and His unfailing love. The book of Ruth is a wonderful story about how one woman's sacrificial love brings about restoration, renewal, and redemption. This little book has only four chapters and eighty-five verses, yet it is filled from beginning to end with nothing but a demonstration of divine love. It is one of only two books of the Bible that have a woman's name as the title. (The book of Esther is the second.) This is the story of a Gentile woman who marries a Jew. It begins with death, but ends with a birth. The late J. Vernon McGee wrote that the book of Ruth is a laboratory demonstration of the 1 Corinthians 13:13 statement: *Now abide faith, hope, love, these three; but the greatest of these is love.*[1] In four short chapters, God begins to unfold His great plan, not only for Ruth and Naomi, but also for our lives as well.

His plan is, first of all, absolutely perfect. Naomi and Ruth had to come to the realization that God's plan was perfect for them. Second, God's plan is a plan of love. Throughout eternity His plan has always emanated from a Father's heart of love for His children. When we're going through difficult circumstances, we so often find it hard to believe that God really loves us. Do you know without a doubt that God loves you and that His plan *for you* is perfect?

Third, God's plan will be fulfilled because God is able. He flung the stars into space and He names them one by one. That very same hand that created the universe also created the seemingly

---

[1] McGee, J. Vernon. *Ruth and Esther: Women of Faith.* Nashville: Thomas Nelson, 1988.

infinite creatures on the earth—over twelve thousand different species of ants, and I probably have had all of them in my kitchen at one time or another!

Fourth, God's plan is always for our good because God is good. His plan is perfect, His plan is loving, and He is able to fulfill it.

I once read the story of a man named Joseph Scriven, who experienced great tragedy in his life. You know how there are times when you think life can't get any worse and then it does? That's how it was for him. And yet, he was a man who was fully dedicated to God's plan no matter what it involved. Right before his wedding day, his wife-to-be drowned when she was thrown from her horse while crossing a bridge. It was a great tragedy and a great loss to him, as it would be for any of us to lose someone we love. Nevertheless, he went on to serve the Lord by ministering to the downtrodden and the outcast all around the world. He later met another woman and planned to make her his bride, but on the eve of their wedding she died of a terrible illness. Joseph Scriven went on to write the hymn, "What a Friend We Have in Jesus." Out of the ashes, mourning, and tragedy of one man's life came this beautiful song that has been sung and beloved for generations.[2]

Similarly, the story of Ruth and Naomi begins with grief and pain, but out of the ashes and tragedy of their lives comes great celebration: *Now it came to pass, in the days when the judges ruled, that there was a famine in the land. And a certain man of Bethlehem, Judah, went to dwell in the country of Moab, he and his wife and his two sons. The name of the man was Elimelech, the name of his wife was Naomi, and the names of his two sons were Mahlon and Chilion—Ephrathites of Bethlehem, Judah. And they went to the country of Moab and remained there* (Ruth 1:1–2).

---

[2] Smith, Jane Stuart, and Carlson, Betty. *Great Christian Hymn Writers*. Wheaton: Crossway, 1997.

Each little word that God has put in the Scriptures is very important. In the *King James Version*, verse 2 says they went *to sojourn* in Moab. What was intended to be a temporary journey became a permanent situation until tragedy struck: *Then Elimelech, Naomi's husband, died; and she was left, and her two sons. Now they took wives of the women of Moab: the name of the one was Orpah, and the name of the other Ruth. And they dwelt there about ten years. Then both Mahlon and Chilion also died; so the woman survived her two sons and her husband.*

Then she arose with her daughters-in-law that she might return from the country of Moab, for she had heard in the country of Moab that the LORD had visited His people by giving them bread. Therefore she went out from the place where she was, and her two daughters-in-law with her; and they went on the way to return to the land of Judah. And Naomi said to her two daughters-in-law, "Go, return each to her mother's house. The LORD deal kindly with you, as you have dealt with the dead and with me. The LORD grant that you may find rest, each in the house of her husband."

Then she kissed them, and they lifted up their voices and wept.

And they said to her, "Surely we will return with you to your people." But Naomi said, "Turn back, my daughters; why will you go with me? Are there still sons in my womb, that they may be your husbands? Turn back, my daughters, go—for I am too old to have a husband. If I should say I have hope, if I should have a husband tonight and should also bear sons, would you wait for them till they were grown? Would you restrain yourselves from having husbands? No, my daughters; for it grieves me very much for your sakes that the hand of the LORD has gone out against me!"

Then they lifted up their voices and wept again; and Orpah kissed her mother-in-law, but Ruth clung to her. And she said, "Look, your sister-in-law has gone back to her people and to her gods; return after your sister-in-law."

But Ruth said: "Entreat me not to leave you, or to turn back from following after you; for wherever you go, I will go; and wherever you lodge, I will lodge; your people shall be my people, and your God, my God. Where you die,

I will die, and there will I be buried. The LORD *do so to me, and more also, if anything but death parts you and me."*

When she saw that she was determined to go with her, she stopped speaking to her. . . . So Naomi returned, and Ruth the Moabitess her daughter-in-law with her, who returned from the country of Moab. Now they came to Bethlehem at the beginning of barley harvest (verses 1:3–18, 22).

What appeared bleak and hopeless was just the beginning of restoration and renewal for their lives, and not only for their lives but for the nation of Israel, and the lives of all generations to come. Ruth 1:1 tells us two important facts. First, it tells us that the judges were ruling. So a time frame is given here. It was a time when Israel had leaders like Deborah, Gideon, and Samson— mighty people who became deliverers in the nation. It was a time of great moral and spiritual decay, as everyone did what was right in his own eyes (Judges 21:25). In fact, if we look around us today, we see that our nation is in a similar state, with sin, moral decay, and injustice all around. Because of Israel's sin, God allowed the people to be in servitude to other nations. He would repeatedly use this discipline to bring them to repentance. In their suffering, they would cry out to God and He would raise up a leader who would bring about their deliverance. But once again they would become complacent and begin the downward spiral into sin. We read in the book of Judges that the nation went through this process of backsliding and deliverance seven times.

Second, verse 1 tells us that there was a famine in the land. As God would seek to discipline the nation and bring about repentance, He would allow other nations to come in and destroy their crops. Famine was the natural outcome. So this family of four—Elimelech, Naomi, Mahlon, and Chilion—was in a difficult situation. Elimelech, seeing his family's need, did what you and I would probably do—he sought to find food for his family.

Even if it meant changing jobs and moving to another community, we would probably do the same. The family left Bethlehem, which means "the house of bread." They went to Moab, which God called His *wash pot*, or *place of refuse* (see Psalm 60:8). They left the *house of bread* for a *place of refuse*.

In this place, Naomi suffered the first of four great losses in her life. She left behind all that was familiar to her and went to a strange heathen land. She left her friends. Have you ever done that? It's really difficult. Or, maybe your friends have left you. That's difficult too. She left her home and possibly all her possessions and servants. I didn't realize how attached I was to my things until I moved back to Costa Mesa from San Diego and my things were in storage for three months! The moment my possessions arrived in the moving van, I realized that I was home. I had felt dispossessed and upset because I wasn't connected to anything around me. How comforting it was to have my things with me again.

Naomi left her place of worship. I imagine she went to the house of God every Sabbath with her husband. We get so accustomed to how wonderful it is to have good fellowship and great teaching. But when we must move, it can be a desert away from our fellowship. It's very difficult, and when we come back, we want to sit and soak in the Word because it brings so much comfort and strength to us. Leaving her place of worship must have been so distressful for Naomi.

She also left her position. Verse 2 tells us that her husband was an Ephrathite. That means he belonged to an upper middle class family and was a man of importance. He was known in the city gates. People greeted them as they walked down the streets of Bethlehem together, but no one knew her when she got to Moab. She was nothing. She was nobody. She was a face in the crowd.

Sometimes you might feel that you're just a face in the crowd. But God has a plan for you as He had a plan for Naomi.

Her second great loss occurred when her husband died. I've been married for forty-seven years and I can't imagine how it would be to lose my husband. Perhaps you have experienced the grief and pain of having your own flesh—the one you are attached to, the one that God gave you all those years ago—snatched away. How tragic that must be. Ironically, these people who had left home to escape death then experienced greater death in the place that was supposed to supply refuge.

Naomi became a single mom in a foreign country. Verse 4 tells us her two precious Jewish boys went out and found Gentile women and brought them into her Jewish home. The Israelites were forbidden to marry Gentiles, and especially not Moabites because they had cruelly treated the Israelites during their exodus from Egypt. Now wouldn't that have been a humiliation and a pain to her? It must have been a terrible heartache to see her sons become unequally yoked.

Perhaps you are watching your children do things that are painful to your heart. There is nothing like grieving over your children who have walked away from the Lord. I watched my own two dear children in their early adult years walk away from the Lord. My son got involved in punk rock music and became addicted to drugs and alcohol. He walked away from everything we had planted in him. It seemed that all we had taught him was thrown back in our faces. I thought, *Lord, why have You allowed this precious son who I love more than my own life to go through this? Why has he done this?* It was a terrible time of grief and pain. But, the story doesn't end there. Both of my children have come back to the Lord and are serving Him. They are now teaching my five precious grandchildren in the ways of the Lord. God is faithful. He used my children's rebellion to teach me many things about waiting on the Lord and He taught me how to pray diligently for them.

Naomi's third great loss occurred when her two sons, Mahlon and Chilion, died. Those names mean "sickly" and "piney," which may tell us something about why they died. Can you imagine naming your two children *Sickly* and *Piney*? You'd be watching them every day to see if they were okay: *Do they have a fever? Am I feeding them right? Don't wander too far because I want to keep my eyes on you.*

Naomi was now not only a widow, she was childless. Think of her devastation—first her husband, and then her two children. I don't think there's a mother who doesn't experience great fear wondering, *What if God takes my child? How will I respond? What will I do?* The Enemy often brings those thoughts, especially to new moms. We see that Naomi, who had gone out full, now was bereft of all that was most precious to her. And in her anguish she must have called out to God many times: *Why God? Why me? Haven't I suffered enough? Am I being punished? Why didn't You take me instead? Why have You forsaken me? What am I to do now? Are You really a God of love to allow all of this tragedy to come upon me?*

Naomi was a woman like us, and when we go through problems that are too difficult and overwhelming for us, those thoughts roll through our mind. Elisabeth Elliot said, *It isn't the problems that determine our destiny. It's how we respond to them. What the caterpillar calls the end of the world the Creator calls a butterfly.*[3] What appeared to Naomi as the end of the world began to turn into a beautiful butterfly because God, in His great love and perfect plan, for Naomi had not left her alone. These two daughters-in-law that had come into her house now became the joy of her heart. She loved them dearly and they

[3] Elliot, Elisabeth. *A Path through Suffering: Discovering the Relationship between God's Mercy and Our Pain.* Ventura: Regal Books, 1990.

loved her passionately. It's interesting that there was this relationship between a mother-in-law and her daughters-in-law. I'm so thankful that I have a wonderful daughter-in-law. If I was to search throughout the universe and take applications, I could never have found a better daughter-in-law than my Lisa. She is awesome, and my son didn't even ask me when he brought her home! He did better than I could have ever imagined. So God, in His wonderful plan, gave to Naomi these two women, Ruth and Orpah, who loved her.

Then, in the midst of her distress, Naomi heard that God had visited His people once more by giving them bread and food back in Bethlehem. Those of you who have experienced tragedy know that when it hits, you long for those things that are most familiar. Your heart and head start turning homeward and you think, *I want to go back. I want to get back to those things that comforted me in the past.* Naomi was in a strange, foreign land where she was an outsider. She longed for her family and friends back home.

When we're confused and things are overwhelming us, we need to go back to the things we know. Pastor Chuck has taught through the years that when you are confused and it seems the whole world is falling in upon you, you need to return to what you do know: *Jesus loves me, this I know, for the Bible tells me so.* Jesus loves me, this I know! If I don't know anything else about the problems, the whys and wherefores, I can be confident that Jesus loves me. Do you know that today? In the midst of your circumstances when the waves and billows are rolling over your head, one after another, do you know that He loves *you* and has a plan for *your* life?

As Naomi made preparations to return to Bethlehem, she suffered her fourth great loss. Verses 14–15 tell us that Orpah, who loved her mother-in-law, kissed her and returned to her own people and her own gods. This is one of the sad-dest points in the whole story because Orpah went back to her gods. One of the gods the Moabites worshipped was the god Chemosh. People would offer their children to this god in sac-rificial fires. What happened to Orpah? I've wondered about this over and over. Did she find a husband when she went back? Did she have her firstborn child? Did she offer that child in sacrifice? She could have made the choice to go with Ruth and Naomi, but she turned back. What a powerful warning for us as believers. Don't ever turn back. If she had followed, she could have experienced all the wonderful blessings that God had in store for Ruth. Orpah professed her love and turned back, but Ruth was the one who possessed true love and fol-lowed it. Ruth's wonderful profession of commitment and faith shows us the true heart of devotion.

Verse 14 says that Ruth clung to Naomi. The *King James Version* says that she *clave*; she stuck closer than glue. The same word is used in Genesis when God tells Adam that he and Eve will become one flesh (see Genesis 2:24). God said that Adam and Eve would cleave together. It's as if the thin pages of our Bible were glued together and then we tried to separate them. What would happen? They would rip apart. Nothing was going to tear Ruth away from her mother-in-law. Naomi gave in and said, *Okay, you can come. Just don't keep hanging on my leg!* Ruth made a clear cutting away of her past to pursue her future with Naomi.

The focus of the story now turns to the providence of God in Ruth's life, and through her life to Naomi. The women returned to Bethlehem at the time of barley harvest. Isn't God wonderful? He's never too early or too late. He knew exactly what time to bring them back so they could be provided for. In chapter 2 we learn that Ruth went into the fields to glean the grains that were left behind by the reapers. This was how the poor were provided for in Israel. Verse 3 says that Ruth *just happened* to come to the field that belonged to Boaz, a relative of Elimelech. Nothing happens with God by chance. It isn't by chance that we land in a particular place at a particular time to fulfill a particular need.

With a denominational background, Jim and I came to Calvary Chapel Costa Mesa in the 1970s simply to be fed the Word. Little did we know that God had placed us here to train us and raise us up in ministry. God was doing a wondrous work— all part of His plan in bringing us here, though we had no idea what would take place when we first came to Calvary Chapel. But God had a plan. He has a plan for you, and He had a plan in bringing Naomi and Ruth back to Bethlehem. It was God's providence at work. J. Vernon McGee said, *Providence is the hand of God in the glove of history. Providence is the means by which God directs all things animate and inanimate, seen and unseen, good and evil toward a worthy purpose—which means that His will must ultimately prevail.*[4] God was working out His plan in the lives of these individuals, but He was also working out His plan for generations to come.

Ruth and Naomi returned to Bethlehem with no visible resources. All they brought was their love for each other and their hope and faith in the provision of God. Jesus said that God has chosen the poor in this world to be rich in faith. He honored Ruth's faith and humility by bringing her to the field of Boaz. He had heard of Ruth's reputation in the city. Don't news and gossip travel fast? Boaz was the first one to give any word of encouragement and comfort to the heart of Ruth. He told his men to keep a special watch over her. As Boaz spotted Ruth across the field, he asked,

---

[4] McGee, J. Vernon. *Thru the Bible Commentary Series: History of Israel: Ezra, Nehemiah, Esther.* Nashville: Thomas Nelson, 1991.

Who is this woman? Once he heard her name, and had a face to put together with the information he had about her character, he fell in love with her at first sight. His heart must have been singing, *The fields are alive with the sound of music!* He was head over heels in love!

Ruth was simply doing what was put in front of her to do—serving her mother-in-law. She was not looking for a husband. That was the farthest thing from her mind. She had five strikes against her when she followed Naomi. First, she was a Gentile. Second, she was a Moabitess. Third, she had been a former heathen idol worshiper. Fourth, she was a widow. Fifth, she was poor; she had no dowry or resources to offer a man. She was absolutely destitute. She was on the same level as a woman today who would be scavenging through the trash for recyclables.

Because Boaz was a near relative of Naomi's husband, he not only had the right to redeem Naomi's property, but the duty by law to marry Ruth and raise up a lineage for her deceased husband. There were three rules concerning this redemption process. (*Redemption* means "to purchase by paying a price.") First, the redeemer had to be a near relative. Second, he had to be personally debt free. Third, he had to be willing to pay the full redemption price. Boaz was more than willing and more than able to meet these conditions because he loved Ruth.

One major problem remained. There was a nearer relative than Boaz, and unless he declined to act as the kinsman redeemer, Boaz and Ruth would not be able to marry. However, God was working in their situation. God's word to Ruth through her mother-in-law in chapter 3, verse 18 was, *Sit still, my daughter, until you know how the matter will turn out; for the man will not rest until he has concluded the matter this day.* Naomi knew the heart of Boaz. The words *sit still* literally mean to "back off and take your hands off the matter." *Stop trying to figure it out. Don't manipulate things. Let God do His work.* Oh, how we like to get our little fingers into situations and try to work everything out. God's plan was in the works and there was nothing on earth that could thwart what God had for these people. Boaz worked all the details out and finally brought Ruth home as his bride.

Warren Wiersbe said, *Ruth went from loneliness to love, from toil to rest, from poverty to wealth, from worry to assurance, and from despair to hope.*[5] Until her marriage to Boaz, Ruth was referred to as *Ruth the Moabitess.* Now, she was no longer called *Ruth the Moabitess,* for the past was gone and she was making a new beginning. As the wife of Boaz, she was given his name, a name she was proud to bear.

Not only was God's providential care evident in the life of Ruth, but God was also fulfilling His plan for Naomi. Boaz and Ruth had a son named Obed, and Obed was a source of joy and comfort to the heart of his grandmother. If you are a grandparent, you know that the joy of having children is being a grandparent. If we could skip parenting and go directly to becoming grandparents, it would be worth it.

Obed continued the family line, and thus protected the family inheritance, which he used to sustain Naomi in her old age. Obed, in God's plan, became the grandfather of Israel's greatest king, David. Through his seed came the King of kings and Lord of lords, Jesus Christ, our Messiah. God's eternal purpose worked out not only in the lives of these people—Ruth, Naomi, and Boaz—but through the generations so that we can also be part of the story of the book of Ruth. This is a great love story: God's plan of love for us.

Ruth is one of only four Gentile women mentioned in the lineage of Jesus Christ. The first was Tamar, who bore children to

---

[5] Wiersbe, Warren. *Be Committed: Doing God's Will Whatever the Cost.* Colorado Springs: Chariot Victor Publishing, 1993.

Judah. The second was Rahab, who let the spies into Jericho. Rahab also happens to be the mother of Boaz. Maybe that's why he loved Ruth. His own mother had been an outsider and an outcast. He looked at Ruth with great compassion because he understood how she felt. The third was Ruth. The fourth, Bathsheba, is mentioned in Matthew chapter 1 in the genealogy of Jesus Christ. She is not mentioned by name, but is referred to as the wife of Uriah.

Four Gentile women in the lineage of Jesus Christ—this shows us that the grace of God was present even in the Old Testament, just as it is available to you and me. We were the outsiders, foreigners, strangers, and pilgrims. We were outside the covenant relationship and God loved us so much that He went to the cross that we might have eternal life. Warren Wiersbe has said, *Too often our concept of God's blessing is bound by time, by wanting visible results now, by our own shortsighted self-centeredness, but God's blessings are shrouded in eternity.*[6]

Think about that. God's blessings are shrouded in eternity. Jesus Christ became our Kinsman Redeemer. He met all the requirements that were necessary for our purchase. First, He became our relative by becoming a man. Second, He was debt free because He committed no sin; He was without spot or blemish. Third, He willingly paid the full redemption price that was required for our purchase; He paid it with His own body and His own blood. There's never been a greater love than God taking on the form of human flesh and laying down His life for you and me.

No one else could fulfill those qualifications except Jesus Christ. His plan from the foundation of the world was always to restore and redeem us. It wasn't Plan B; it was always Plan A. Just as God took Ruth and Naomi from great poverty to great prosperity, God wants to take us from our spiritual poverty into great

---

[6] Ibid.

spiritual prosperity. He wants us to experience the wealth that can only come from knowing Jesus Christ in a personal and real way.

Reflections

1. Take a moment and reflect on the story of Ruth and Naomi.
2. What is your immediate response to its spiritual lessons?
3. Does this story bring to light any areas of needed repentance in your life? Be specific.
4. How does God's great love and provision for Ruth and Naomi cause you to remember His great love and provision for you? List examples from your own life.
5. Renew your commitment to your Kinsman Redeemer by writing a prayer of thanksgiving and praise for all He has done.

About the Author

June Hesterly accepted Christ when she was seven years old. She has been married for forty-seven years and is the mother of two married children, and grandmother to five incredible grandchildren. She came to Calvary Chapel Costa Mesa in the early days when the church met in a small chapel on Sunflower Avenue.

June has served in ministry for thirty-five years. She and her husband Jim planted and pastored a Calvary Chapel in the San Diego area before returning to Costa Mesa several years ago. June is a retreat and conference speaker and has served on the pastors' wives retreat board since its inception. She also serves on the Joyful Life Bible study board at Calvary Chapel Costa Mesa. She has traveled throughout the world with Jim, director of Acts 1:8 Ministry, speaking about the gifts of the Holy Spirit and other topics. They have co-authored three study guides for Pastor Chuck Smith's books, along with a pamphlet on the baptism of the Holy Spirit. June is also the author of a retreat planning guide.